T0118537

Judy R. De Wit

FORGIVING THE CHURCH

How to Release
the Confusion and Hurt
when the Church Abuses

iUniverse, Inc.
Bloomington

Forgiving the Church
How to Release the Confusion and Hurt
when the Church Abuses

iUniverse books may be ordered through booksellers or by contacting:

iUniverse
1663 Liberty Drive
Bloomington, IN 47403
www.iuniverse.com
1-800-Authors (1-800-288-4677)

ISBN: 978-1-4620-5906-5 (sc)
ISBN: 978-1-4620-5907-2 (e)

Printed in the United States of America

iUniverse rev. date: 11/11/2011

Contents

Acknowledgments   xiii
Note from the Author   xv
Introduction   xvii

Chapter 1   Remembering the Church of My Childhood   1
Chapter 2   Determining Our Beliefs about Church   5
Chapter 3   Abuse and Its Effects: In Our Homes
            and Families   8
Chapter 4   Abuse and Its Effects: In Our Churches   20
Chapter 5   Stories of Abuse and Its Effects: In the
            Christian Environment   32
Chapter 6   More Stories of Abuse in the Church   45
Chapter 7   Forgiving: What the Church Should Do
            (And What If the Church Doesn't)   52
Chapter 8   Forgiving: What the Victim Should Do   64
Chapter 9   Putting it All Together: Forgiving the
            Church   73

Bibliography   79

Forgiving the Church

Revenge may seem sweet but only true forgiveness can bring lasting peace. Judy De Wit reminds us that hope for the future is found when we deal with the hurts of the past. The pain of abuse is found in every corner of the church. When church leaders abuse, trust is shattered. When the healers bring hurt, lives are devastated. Healing comes in forgiveness. Judy walks the reader from the depths of the pain to the joy of freedom in Christ who died to make forgiveness possible.

Rev. Jerry Dykstra
Former Executive Director
of the Christian Reformed Church

Judy De Wit has a gift for writing in a very clear, comprehensive, and coherent way that allows the reader to get right to the heart of the issue. Abuse at the hand of someone in church authority can be heartbreaking, confusing, and spiritually debilitating. *Forgiving the Church* is a manual for working through the consequences of abuse and the processes of forgiveness.

Dr. Melissa Baartman Mork, PsyD
Northwestern College, St. Paul, MN

Foreword

Perhaps there is no better place to define the concept of forgiveness than in the subject of church leader abuse in the churches. While abuse in the church needs to be dealt with in a just manner, the church also needs to understand, promote, and practice the biblical concept of forgiveness.

In her follow up to her book *Breaking the Silence within the Church: Responding to Abuse Allegations*, in *Forgiving the Church: How to Release the Confusion and Hurt when the Church Abuses*, Judy De Wit moves to the subject of forgiveness for the victims of abuse. Already within the title of her new book Judy helps define forgiveness in the words of the title "*How to release the confusion and hurt when the church abuses.*" In her book, Judy aptly points out the danger inherent within people's ignorant and misguided concepts of the term forgiveness that is tied to the cliché "forgive and forget" which rather than providing release and healing tends to diminish the sin and even indict the victim rather than the offender.

In order to rightly set the stage for defining and leading victims and the church through the forgiveness process, De Wit begins by describing the experience of one who is raised in the church where a strong sense of honor, respect, and obedience was given to leaders so that one assumed that they are trustworthy and truly represent the just and loving God to whom they must answer. But when one realizes that church leadership is made up of people prone to sin like everybody else, one begins to rightly ask the question when and how it is appropriate to challenge those in authority, both in terms of what they teach and in light of their behavior, especially when they violate their offices. In order to help the reader process their reflection on their church experience, De Wit then describes abuse and its effects on people in their homes and churches. She identifies types of abuse in both settings everywhere from child sexual abuse to lesser forms of abuse such as clergy malpractice and invasion of privacy. In identifying the types of abuse, she provides explanation for each category. By including a broader understanding of abuse she states in the final paragraph of Chapter 4: *"Although sexual abuse by clergy is the most damaging and horrendous of all the abuses, know that the understanding of abuse in a broader sense is also what brings harm to people and mars the name of Christ."* She then gives a number of real-life stories of abuse that have taken place in the church or "Christian environment" that demonstrate both the types of abuse as well as their effects on the victims and churches.

With the types of abuse defined, she then finally moves to what the church and victims must do to facilitate the forgiving process in chapters 7 and 8. Here the subject of forgiveness is clearly described as a process that requires the cooperation and just actions by church leaders working with victims through the process so as to make sure that biblical justice, pastoral care, accountability, and genuine healing takes place. Again, De Wit's own words show that the church's "governing authorities must do their part to make forgiveness for the victim possible" (conclusion of chapter 7). She then moves to what the victim herself must do in chapter 8. Here again, the process of forgiveness is shown to be one in which everybody involved must truly understand what forgiveness is and what it is not. Likewise, for the victim and the church, the forgiveness process is difficult. It is "hard work" that requires careful attention to thought, feeling, appropriate action, and the willingness to be helped by others through the process. She closes chapter 8 by adding that it requires time, prayer and patience. *"With God's help you can do it."*

De Wit closes the book with a chapter on taking all the issues raised in the earlier chapters and then "putting it all together" by asking a very appropriate question. "Why?" Why should someone who did not ask to be abused in the first place, who has already struggled so much with its consequences in her life, even bother to forgive the church, let alone the abuser? She answers by saying "Because God says so," again applying appropriate Scripture passages. Likewise, "So the abuse stops abusing," "So bitterness is prevented," and finally, "Because it's what's best for us."

As with her previous book, I really appreciate De Wit's passionate and careful attention to the hard details that the church sadly tends to avoid, not only in terms of abuse of leaders but also in disciplining its members in learning to forgive one another in all cases of offense. As with subject of love the church tends to treat forgiveness as something easy to do but also will misuse it to avoid the painful work of strengthening the body of Christ through facing the ugliness of our sin and bring genuine reconciliation to deep divisions caused by sin in the body.

As a pastor and, previously, a member of specialized abuse ministries in my denomination, I have witnessed both the damaging effects of abuse on members of the church and the church itself. I have also been privy to a painful reconciliation within a church family. But I also have felt the frustration of ignorance and sloppy efforts of my own and others to bring about this needed healing. It forces me to ask the question, "Do I really know what forgiveness is and how to bring it about?"

Forgiving the Church is an excellent resource to help church leaders navigate through the "messiness" of abuse and Christ's requirement that we forgive one another in a God-honoring way. As in her previous work, De Wit offers a pathway through the murky and unpleasant minefield that abuse in the church presents to us all. Victims need help. The churches need help. It's time for the church to practice Christ-like ministry and to "release the confusion and hurt when the church abuses." In other words, we really need to practice Godly forgiveness. This book definitely will help the church do that!

Rev. Harrison Newhouse
Hancock Christian Reformed Church
Hancock, Minnesota

Acknowledgments

To the many victims of church leadership abuse: you are my inspiration to write this book.

You have suffered much. You have been re-victimized and re-traumatized in your efforts to be heard by your church. Your re-abuse experiences grieve my heart, and my prayers and love go out to you as you search for continued healing and recovery.

Special acknowledgment goes to those of you who have been willing to hear and process my concerns regarding abuse in the church, and more specifically to those who belong to the Christian Reformed Church.

Sincere thanks to:

Rev. Jerry Dykstra, for your willingness to let me process my frustrations and anger about the abuse that happens in the CRC and for your pastoral care side that shows genuine concern about abuse in the CRC.

Dr. Melissa Mork, for your encouragement and support for my writing of a second book. Your expertise is always appreciated.

Rev. Harrison Newhouse, for your encouragement in my work for the CRC and for your support when my frustrations reach their limit.

Dr. Jana Reinhart, whose inspiration and encouragement helped me complete this book.

The counseling staff at Nystrom and Associates, Ltd., of New Brighton, MN, who provide ongoing encouragement and prayers for the work I do for victims abused by the church.

God, who gave me the words to make writing this book possible and provided me with the determination to see it completed.

Judy R. De Wit

Note from the Author

The purpose of my first book, *Breaking the Silence within the Church*, was to help councils and elder boards to know what to do when abuse allegations against a church leader come forward. After seeing church leaders struggling with how to respond to complainants alleging abuse by a church leader, I was led by God to give a step-by-step process that could help any church and congregation faced with such a challenge.

Now I hear God's call again. This time He tugged at my heart to write something to help victims who have been abused by a church leader. *Forgiving the Church* is a book for those who have been abused by the church but don't know how to forgive. The book spells out the different kinds of abuse in the church, the kinds of action councils/elder boards should take when allegations come forward, and the steps that should be taken to help the victim and others forgive when the church abuses.

Abuse has horrendous effects. When the abuse is committed by a church leader, the damage multiplies exponentially. The church has a spiritual responsibility to support and help its victims and abusers through the healing and recovery times. This book gives guidance on how to forgive the church.

Judy R. De Wit

Introduction

The Christian Reformed Church and other denominations have struggled for many years with understanding the topic of abuse, what it looks like, and how to respond to it.

In the mid-eighties, and then into the nineties, the Roman Catholic Church was inundated with sexual abuse allegations. Victims came forward and told stories of how they were sexually abused and assaulted by priests. What had once been covered up by bishops now became exposed and public for the entire world to hear. Truth, apologies, restitution, and compensation were demanded as the victims told how their lives had been destroyed by what the leaders of the Catholic Church had done. As the public watched and heard the horrendous stories of these victims, we as Christians grieved and became enraged with them at the thought of church leaders doing such things.

At the same time, a similar thing happened in a church I know well. A woman from the congregation had been hurt by her pastor soon after his arrival to the church. When the allegations about what the pastor had done became public, the church leaders were quick to try to silence the victim and call the victim a liar—and they allowed the pastor to keep his position. The victim ran away in the hurt of it all, the church members were confused about what happened, and everyone lost in the end.

Abuse by the church needs to become a central concern for all members of the Christian church. Christ established the church to bring healing and grace to a hurting and broken world. He gave us the ministry of reconciliation. He never intended for His church to become a place of harm and destruction. Set apart and mandated, Christ calls His church to nurture and love others and to be a healing agent in a broken world.

So when the church sins against us, how do we begin the forgiveness process?

Forgiving the Church begins by asking us to remember the church of our childhood. When we are young, we are easily impressed and impacted by the world around us. We believe that adults know everything, that we must do whatever they say, and that they are always right. That same thing happens with the church. When we are young, we trust that what the church says and does is right. We believe church leaders know everything and that they are special because they are "from God." What we believe about church today was formed when we were children.

When we become adults, we explore what beliefs we have about the church and church leaders. Do church leaders really know how to lead a church? Do we really trust them? Do they ever make mistakes? If church leaders make mistakes, how should that be addressed? Should church leaders be confronted about their sins the way the church members sitting in the pews are? What should be done when church leaders commit moral failure?

Abuse is real in our homes, churches, and society. But are we sure we know what abuse is? *Forgiving the Church* explores what abuse looks like in our homes, then proceeds by explaining what abuse looks like in the context of the church.

This book shares many stories of abuse both in the home and in the church. As you read through the various scenarios, you will begin to see how abuse within our families and abuse by church leaders are very similar.

Building on this foundation, we are ready to begin the discussion of how to forgive the church.

Forgiving the church is a twofold process. One crucial issue is that the church should help the victim when she comes forward with her allegations. By ensuring a safe and appropriate process for the victim, the church will be helping her start the forgiveness process.

Second, she is the one who can choose to forgive. Forgiveness is not an easy or quick process. In fact, it can take years, even decades. Forgiving the church may be one of the most difficult things the victim will ever have to do. This book will provide guidance to help begin the process of forgiving and advice to help the victim begin the "letting go" of the shame, hurt, and guilt that accompanies victims who are abused by the church.

There are many books that provide excellent information about forgiveness—the theology of why and what we should do. *Forgiving the Church* has a different approach. Its focus is on empowering church leaders to do their part in responding to abuse so that victims can do their part and begin the process of forgiving the church.

Judy R. De Wit

Chapter 1
Remembering the Church of My Childhood

Train up a child in the way he should go. And when he is old he will not depart from it.

—Proverbs 22:6

It was a large white wooden church located in a small rural town in Northwest Iowa. It had large gothic style windows on each of its sides and there were lots of steps to climb before reaching the two main entrances on the south side. With a slanting, time-worn aisle, creaky hard benches, and a pipe organ that could awaken any snoozer, this church of my childhood holds many fond and sometimes confusing memories.

At the front of the church, there was a piano on one side of the platform and an organ on the other. On the platform, there were what looked like hard chairs on either side of the pulpit. I often wondered how comfortable those chairs were, because it seemed that when the pastor sat on them, they were as hard as the creaky bench I was sitting on. Behind the platform was a large wooden backdrop that hid the pipes of the big pipe organ. Along the top of the edge of the backdrop were stenciled the words "Enter His Gates with Thanksgiving and His Courts with Praise." I always liked that verse. It made sense to me.

My church had a large gallery where we as a family would sometimes sit. My dad used to be an usher and the family always sat in the very back bench when he ushered. Of course, I was too little to really see anything way down in front, but that really didn't matter.

Church was always hot in the summer, but we never missed a service. We would sit on the side so we could maybe get a bit of a breeze from the windows. Some families sat right in the front to be by the two big fans that were running. We always took our little handheld fans along to cool ourselves.

I can remember certain families in my "growing-up" church. There was one elderly couple who always sat on the "west" side of the church. They had an adult handicapped son with them. I remember Mom talking about how he "wasn't right" and saying that his parents didn't take him out in public very much. I always felt sorry for him and wondered if he had friends. Another family I remember had eight kids. I was often amazed when I watched this family come into church because they took nearly the entire bench. And there was another family who had a girl who was deaf. Her family usually sat in the back of church so her mom could sign the church service to her. Eventually I became friends with her.

On the right side of the platform there was a "consistory" door, out of which a line of men dressed in black suits and white shirts would file, about five minutes before church started. Behind that door was the consistory room. And sometimes, if someone unexpectedly opened the consistory door before church started, I could see the men sitting in the consistory room waiting for church to start.

Things ran like clockwork in this church. At exactly five minutes before the church service began, usually around the same time the organist began to play, the line of consistory members would file out of the consistory door and sit about five benches from the front of church. Their reserved bench was a puzzle for me. I guess I couldn't understand why my family had to come twenty minutes early to get a good seat in the back while others could come in five minutes before the service and get a reserved seat.

I had a little girl's understanding of what the elders were supposed to do. I couldn't understand how a row of men could "watch" me if they sat in front of me. I doubted that any of them really knew me. So if they didn't know me, how could they ever be a help to me?

I was taught to fear the elders of the church. They were very important and I was to respect and obey them. However, most of them were farmers, and I had a hard time understanding how they could lead the church and farm at the same time. For me, a leader who spent most of his time in barns and on tractors couldn't be connecting that much to church.

I often wondered what the elders talked about in that consistory room. It's not that they were unfriendly to me, just distant. I sometimes wondered why they weren't more interested in who I was or what I thought. I wondered if they really cared about all of the questions I had about God and religion.

Two elders from my church came to our house once a year for "church visiting." On the day they were scheduled to come, I can remember my mom fussing about things. She made sure the house was especially clean, made sure we knew which text we were supposed to read before they came, and made sure there was a special lunch if we were the last family they were visiting for the evening. She gave us many instructions about how we should behave while they were here. The visits were generally quiet and composed—almost somber. I have no memory of laughing and enjoying the interactions.

It was an especially big deal if the two visitors who came were an elder and the pastor. Somehow having the pastor at the house caused additional stress for my parents. I suppose it was important to impress the pastor because he was the most educated man in the community. I knew it was important not to mess up when the elders and the pastor were around.

The church of my childhood seemed to have a lot of rules. It was important to know the rules and follow them. It seemed that the rules mostly were about how I was to behave while in church, how I was supposed "to be" in the community, and how I was supposed to follow all of the dos and don'ts the Bible talks about. The authority of the church leaders was held in the highest regard, and I can remember many sermons about "obeying" the leadership of the church. Messages about not challenging the church leaders were clear; their authority meant they knew best. As a young teen, I once asked the pastor during catechism class what he thought would happen if someone found one of the doctrines of our church to be in conflict with the teaching of the Bible. He assured me that such matters would be examined carefully. I think I was challenging the church and the leaders' belief that "we do everything right around here." I wanted to know what would happen if it were not so.

Our memories and experiences of the church we grew up in create powerful beliefs about what the church is and what it's supposed to be. I challenge you to take a few moments and bring to mind what you remember about your growing-up church. Those experiences form and shape your beliefs and expectations about what church should be today.

Chapter 2
Determining Our Beliefs about Church

Obey your leaders and submit to their authority. They keep watch over you as men who must give an account.

—Hebrews 13: 17

We are easily influenced and impacted by the events and people of our childhood. What we see, hear, and experience as children becomes what we know and therefore come to believe to be true as adults. As children, because we are in our formative years and are easily impressed by what adults tell us, we believe what we're told is true. If we are told that hard work is the only thing that matters, we come to believe that's true. If we're told that good Christians should live at peace with others no matter what the cost, we do that. And sadly, if we're told as children that we will never amount to much of anything, we grow up believing that.

It's only when we get older that we start to see things differently. We realize that many things that seemed black and white when we were children become very gray as we entered our teens and twenties. We begin to recognize the inconsistencies in how adults do things. We realize that adults don't know everything. We see that our parents have their own blind spots. The belief that adults—and especially our parents—know everything and don't make mistakes changes as we age and mature.

This also happens to us in the context of the church. What we thought to be true about the church when we were children becomes open to question as we get older. We may once have thought there was one way to do things, but now we have reservations. Is there, for example, a more meaningful way to worship? Can expressing our feelings about God and giving personal testimonies in church benefit and edify us spiritually? Can having a band, using worship leaders, and singing contemporary songs deepen our worship service? These are important questions to ask.

However, there are other questions that need to be asked with regard to the function and leadership of the church. What do we believe about the roles and responsibilities of pastors, youth leaders, church leaders, and council members? What can they do and not do? Are they ever wrong? Where do our beliefs about their leadership style come from? Are those beliefs accurate and true? What does it mean when we say they are called by God and we must submit to their authority? Is there ever a time for us to challenge their approach to leadership? If so, when? How do we challenge their leadership appropriately? Do we obey them simply because they are the leaders of the church or should we be using our own education and knowledge to challenge them when they have strayed from doing what is right?

There is more to ponder. What happens when church leadership fails and does harm instead of good? What about moral failure on the part of a pastor or church leader? What if a church leader is abusive or a church board is harsh and gives poor counsel? How should such matters be addressed? If we cling to our childhood beliefs about church and church leadership, believing that our leaders are right and good and that we are to submit to them in all things, how do we respond when they wrong us? Are we supposed to forgive and forget? Should we ignore and minimize their wrongful behavior? Should we use a standard of discipline different from that we use for the members of the church? Should the leaders who wrong us be directed to step down from their position of authority and have their power relinquished?

What about the victims of the wrongful and abusive behavior of a pastor or leader? How do we treat them? Do we shun them and ostracize them to get them to be quiet? Do we believe them? How do we respond? What about "forgive and forget"? Are they entitled to an apology? And if so, what kind of apology should it be? What about compensation, restitution, and addressing the financial obligations that the victim might face because of the wrongful and abusive acts? Who should know about what happened?

And more. What about forgiveness? Does a person have to forgive a church leader or pastor when he or she has abused? And if so, how? What needs to be done on behalf of the church administration so that victims can forgive abusive leaders? What do victims need in the aftermath of being abused by a church leader? What do victims need in order to forgive a church leader?

Let's see if we can find answers to these questions.

Chapter 3
Abuse and Its Effects: In Our Homes and Families

The tongue that brings healing is a tree of life, but a hurtful tongue crushes the spirit.

—Prov. 15:4

"Anna" (not her real name) tells how her stepdad would do bad things to her when Mom was at work. Starting when she was just eight years old, her stepdad would fondle her and force her to perform oral sex. He threatened her and told her not to tell anyone, and he convinced her that this was a way fathers showed love to their daughters.

By the time she reached her early teen years, she knew it had to stop. She told the school counselor what was going on. When her mom realized what was happening, she asked the judge for a restraining order and divorced her husband soon afterward. Eventually, he was arrested and sentenced to prison. Anna never saw her stepfather again.

With tears in her eyes, she recounts the times she tried to lock her bedroom door so he wouldn't be able to come in at night. She tells how she tried to protect herself by asking to stay at a friend's house when she knew stepdad and she would be home alone. She remembers very little about her childhood except that she felt afraid and she dreaded going home after school.

She admits that her childhood abuse has affected her marriage. She fears intimacy and has a difficult time trusting others. She knows that she lies and distorts things that are happening and sometimes manipulates others so that things go her way. Although she knows she does these things, she feels powerless to change. She reports that her emotions frequently implode and explode. Her greatest desire is to find peace and solitude in her life.

Abuse in our Christian homes is real. It may have happened to you or someone who is close to you. Its effects are long-lasting and devastating. Even those victims who have received the needed therapy for recovery continue to struggle daily with feelings of incompleteness and inadequacy.

We are familiar with the many kinds of abuse—sexual and physical abuse, emotional and verbal abuse, domestic violence, family violence, sexual assault, child abuse, spiritual abuse, and abuse by a church leader. Abuse in whatever form has a variety of effects on its victims. Let's explore these different kinds of abuse and their effects.

Child Sexual abuse

According to the National Center for Victims of Crime (2011), sexual assault takes many forms including attacks such as rape or attempted rape, as well as any unwanted sexual contact or threats. Usually a sexual assault occurs when someone touches any part of another person's body in a sexual way, even through clothes, without that person's consent. Some types of sexual acts which fall under the category of sexual assault include forced sexual intercourse (rape), sodomy (oral or anal sexual acts), child molestation, incest, fondling and attempted rape. Sexual assault in any form is often a devastating crime. Assailants can be strangers, acquaintances, friends, or family members. Assailants commit sexual assault by way of violence, threats, coercion, manipulation, pressure or tricks. Whatever the circumstances, no one asks or deserves to be sexually assaulted.

Sexual abuse of anyone, but especially a minor, is a criminal act. Authorities will investigate situations in which a minor is touched in the private areas, whether or not the touch is outside or under clothing. When it becomes known, this criminal activity must be reported to child protection services or to the local police authorities. Other acts that will incur criminal charges include forcing children to watch pornographic materials or witness sex acts that occur between two adults, or exposing children to sexually explicit material.

Anyone can report child abuse. Certain professionals are required to report child sexual abuse. Information regarding who is considered a mandated reporter for your state can be obtained by contacting your state offices. Schoolteachers, doctors, nurses, medical personnel, therapists, counselors, police officers, attorneys, and pastors are typically required to report abuse they suspect or become aware of.

If a mandated reporter fails to report child sexual abuse that is known to him or her, there can be fines and even jail time for this negligence. For example, in the state of Minnesota, a pastor has twenty-four hours to report child abuse to the county authorities when it becomes known to him or her. The penalty for failing to do so is a large fine and/or jail time.

Effects of childhood sexual abuse

Sexual abuse of a minor causes a tremendous amount of damage. The extent of that damage can vary depending on the how/when/who aspects of the abuse. Ainscough and Toon (2000) state that the damage and the effects of childhood sexual abuse depend on several factors, including:

- Who the abuser was
- How many abusers were involved
- If the abuser was the same sex or the opposite sex as the victim
- What took place
- What was said
- How long the abuse lasted
- How the child felt and how he or she interpreted what was happening
- If the child was otherwise happy and supported
- How other people reacted to the disclosure or discovery of the abuse
- How old the child was

(p. 38)

The damage done to one victim can be quite different from that suffered by another. If the child was abused once, the damage done to that child will be quite different from that inflicted on a child who has been abused for many years. If the abuse occurred when the child was five years old, the extent of the damage is quite different from the trauma experienced by a child who was abused at age thirteen. If one victim has been abused by her stepfather while another was abused by a cousin who was two years older, the effects of the abuse are not the same. If the child reported the abuse and it was believed, the damage will be much different than if the child was ridiculed for making such a report.

Allender (1990) divides the effects of childhood sexual abuse into three main categories. The first is the *powerlessness* felt because the victim was robbed of the freedom to choose. This powerlessness leads the victim to feel as a sense of emptiness, helplessness, and the relentless pain of the soul which leads to even more damage and manifests as self-doubt, despair, and deadness. As the loss of a sense of self and the loss of a sense of judgment occurs, the victim no longer knows who he or she really is. This loss of identity is accompanied by feelings of incompleteness (pp. 113–126).

Feelings of *betrayal* are core to the damage done by childhood sexual abuse (Allender, 1990). Trust and respect for one another are the cores to building relationships. When relationships are not built on foundations of trust and respect for one another, the healthy understanding of what relationships are supposed to be is destroyed. The betrayal of parents who abuse their children instead of nurturing them, the grooming tactics of a perpetrator that create confusion about who to trust and not trust, and the failure of parents to protect their children from abuse all set the groundwork for children never knowing what a healthy relationship really looks like (pp. 127–141).

The third effect of childhood sexual abuse is *ambivalence* (Allender, 1990). Ambivalence in this context is defined by Allender as "feeling two contradictory emotions at the same moment" (143). The abuse may have caused contradictory feelings of pleasure and excitement for what was happening as well as feelings of shame and confusion. As Allender explains, "Central to understanding ambivalence is the fact that the very thing that was despised also brought some degree of pleasure" (p. 146). These conflicting emotions can rage within the soul of the victim and later, as adults, result in anguish caused by their bodies or soul having betrayed them (p.146).

In many years of clinical practice, victims of abuse have shared many other effects of sexual abuse, including experience anxiety, panic attacks, suicidal ideation, inappropriate guilt, shame, depression, sleep problems, nightmares, a need to control, trust issues, and have difficulty saying "no" to sex. Some speak of sexual aggression, identity problems, sexual orientation issues, and marital problems. Frequently, abuse issues interfere with a victim's ability to concentrate at work, to the point that his or her work performance is affected, even to the point of being dismissed from his or her position.

Victims of childhood sexual abuse have difficulty recalling

any experiences from their childhood. When asked about what their elementary schools looked like or who their teachers were, they can't remember. When asked about Christmases or where they went on summer vacations, nothing comes to mind. They have no memories of childhood birthdays.

Victims of childhood sexual abuse have typical dysfunctional patterns of interactions with adults. They often have a history of high-conflict relationships with family and friends. They admit to their need to manipulate and control others so they can control what goes on around them. They know they lie and distort and they admit they do it so that they can feel good about themselves. When asked about their abandonment and rejection issues, they admit their emotions are easily triggered when they are rejected as adults. They tell how they like to create drama because being the center of attention is important to them.

With their fragmented and lost childhoods, victims of childhood sexual abuse weep over how the abuse has robbed them of everything.

Adult sexual assault

The website of the Office of Crimes Victims Advocacy describes sexual assault in this way:

> Most often when people hear the words "sexual assault" they think of rape ... While it is true that rape by a stranger is a form of sexual assault, it is vital to include the wide range of unwanted sexual contacts that many people experience in our definition of these words. Sexual assault can include child sexual abuse, rape, attempted rape, incest, exhibitionism, voyeurism, obscene phone calls, fondling, and sexual harassment.

The site goes on to define rape as "any sexual intercourse with a person without his or her consent. It is an act of violence that uses sex as a weapon." There are different kinds of rape. When someone is raped and she (or he) does not know who the offender is, it's called stranger rape. Acquaintance rape is when the victim and the perpetrator know each other. Date rape is a kind of acquaintance rape where one person rapes the other while in a dating relationship. Marital rape happens between a husband and wife.

Sexual harassment is described by the Office of Crimes Victims Advocacy as "any unwelcome sexual advances, requests for sexual favors, and other verbal or physical conduct of a sexual nature. Sexual harassment often manifests itself in subtle ways, such as sexually suggestive comments, unwanted touching, risqué jokes, or blatant demand for sexual contact."

Discussion of sexual harassment usually centers on the workplace, but sexual harassment can happen anywhere. When someone tells you that he dreamed about having sex with you or someone sends you text messages and pictures that are inappropriate, sexual harassment is happening. Or if someone says that he wants a favor done in exchange for sex, sexual harassment has occurred.

Effects of adult sexual assault

There are many effects of sexual assault. Victims share in session that they suffer from flashbacks, nightmares, and difficulty with sleep; experience times of raging, implosions, and explosions; can't concentrate, experience anxiety and panic attacks, suffer from excessive self-blame, guilt, and shame, and have physical health problems.

Victims of adult sexual assault live in fear. They fear that an assault will happen again. This fear often controls them, and they become obsessed with their safety. They are on near constant watch for someone who may be watching them or following them or may attack them. Their fears of safety often cause them to stay indoors most of the time with their doors locked. And in the night, they have difficulty sleeping, sensing that someone is trying to get in or someone is in the room with them.

Victims of adult sexual assault live in fear of intimacy. Even with someone who is safe, they find it difficult to allow themselves to be vulnerable to another, worrying that they will be controlled by the other. Sharing themselves with another brings back the experience of the assault. This causes them to experience high anxiety and panic, robbing them of the joy that an appropriate sexual experience can bring.

Victims of adult sexual assault have problems with trust. Although they desire closeness with someone, they question whether they can really trust a person who is becoming emotionally close to them. Fears—that they will be harmed, that they will be betrayed again, or that they will be abandoned— cause them to pull back from the relationship. This drawing close and then pulling back creates confusion for those who want to be close to them.

Physical, emotional, and verbal abuse of children

The National Center on Child Abuse and Neglect define and give examples of child physical abuse on the website findcounseling.com. Child physical abuse is:

> The physical injury or maltreatment of a child under the age of eighteen by a person who is responsible for the child's welfare under circumstances which indicate that the child's health or welfare is harmed or threatened. [Examples of physical abuse include] beating with a belt, shoe, or other object; biting a child; breaking a child's arm, leg, or other bones; burning a child with matches or cigarettes; hitting a child; kicking a child; not letting a child eat, drink, or use the bathroom; pulling a child's hair out; punching a child; scalding a child with water that is too hot; shaking, shoving, or slapping a child.

It would be safe to say that if contact with a child results in a mark or bruise remains on a child that is not the result of an accident, it would be classified as abuse. The authorities who investigate physical abuse of children are looking for a mark left on the child.

Emotional abuse is a part of all forms of child abuse and is divided into categories by MedicineNet.com. These categories include:

- rejecting (for example, refusing to acknowledge the child's worth and emotional needs)
- isolation (denying the child social experiences: locking child in the closet is an extreme example)
- terrorizing (verbal assault with or without weapons)
- ignoring (refusing to show affection)
- corrupting (reinforcing destructive, antisocial, or sexually exploitative behaviors)
- verbal assault (extreme sarcasm, name calling, public humiliation)
- over-pressuring (criticism of age-appropriate behaviors/skills as inadequate)

Emotional abuse does a great deal of damage. It eats at the core of who the person is and does damage to the sense of self. Throughout the years of emotional abuse, children come to believe what they have been told: they are worthless, will never amount to anything, and don't deserve anything good. Because of that, they live in the belief that they have to earn love. They are busy trying to be extra good to those around them in the hope that someone will accept and approve of them. Desiring deeply to belong, they will do nearly anything to get someone to love them. They are driven by a need to earn love, believing that no one could actually love them just because of who they are.

Effects of physical, emotional, and verbal abuse of children

The physical, emotional, and verbal abuse of children has long-lasting effects. Victims of this kind of abuse experience anxiety and panic attacks, depression, poor concentration, self-esteem and self-confidence issues, suicidal thoughts, headaches, stomach aches, sleeping problems, eating disorders, and separation anxiety.

Children who grew up in physically and emotionally abusive homes come to believe that they have little to no value and can't do anything right. They believe they are worthless and hopeless, and the messages from their parents linger in their minds as they struggle to find value in themselves as adults. In their efforts to try to prove themselves, they are driven to try and try again, hoping that someone will notice they are capable of doing things. They cling to the thought that maybe, just maybe, Dad and Mom may finally give their approval if they try hard enough.

Domestic violence and adult emotional and verbal abuse

Those who have been physically abused know the pain of being hit, having objects thrown at them, or being thrown up against the wall. Victims of domestic violence either take the abuse, believing they deserve it, or run and hide. Bruised and scratched, they tell their therapists they can't leave because there is nowhere to go. They say that they are bad and the marriage problems are their fault, because they have not tried hard enough or they are stupid. Convinced that the therapists will again blame them for not trying hard enough, they are unable to hear the words that they need to call the police.

Emotional abuse and verbal abuse have many similar effects. When the controller uses yelling, shame, blame, name-calling, and demeaning messages to the spouse, emotional and verbal abuse has occurred. Abusers use isolation and intimidation with their spouses as a way to control them. They demand explanations about how money is spent and require proof of receipts to ensure they are telling the truth. A woman who lives with an abusive husband is quick to blame herself for anything that goes wrong. Because of this, her life becomes extremely anxious; she always fears the next mistake she will make.

Effects of domestic violence and adult emotional and verbal abuse

Some of the effects of domestic violence, including emotional and verbal abuse, are anxiety, chronic pain and depression, dissociative states, drug and alcohol dependence, eating disorders, emotional overreactions to stimuli, general emotional numbing, health problems, panic attacks, poor adherence to medical recommendations, repeated self-injury, self-neglect, sexual dysfunction, sleep disorders, strained family relationships, suicide attempts, and an inability to adequately respond to the needs of their children (findcounseling.com).

Women in abusive relationships have difficulty knowing and admitting the truth about what is happening to them. They blame themselves for the abuse; the abuser has trained them to believe that it is their fault. Fearful of leaving (either because they are afraid their abusers will come after them or they have no place to go), women in abusive relationships tend to stay with their abusers. Abusers have convinced their wives or girlfriends that they are shameful people and deserve the abuse they get. The cycle of abuse, remorse, and reconciling is never-ending. Each time the abuser promises that it won't happen again, the victim believes him and gives him another chance.

Conclusion

Abuse always robs. It always ruins, always destroys, and always hurts. From nightmares to anxiety to a need to control to mistrust, abuse does so much damage to one's ability to handle life. What God intended for us to enjoy, abuse destroys. Trust, love, and respect for one another become distrust, hate, harm, violence, and destruction.

Our Christian homes are no exception. We would like to think that it doesn't happen to us or to anyone we know, but that is not true. It has happened and is happening to those we know and love. I cannot count the number of times fellow Christians and church members have shared their stories of abuse in their marriages and families. Sadly, and too many times, our response has not been enough.

Chapter 4
Abuse and Its Effects: In Our Churches

Rescue me, O Lord, from evil men; protect me from men of violence, who devise evil plans in their hearts and stir up war every day. They make their tongues as sharp as a serpent's; the poison of vipers is on their lips. Keep me, O Lord, from the hands of the wicked; protect me from men of violence who plan to trip my feet.

—Ps. 140:1–4

Sexual abuse is the most horrendous of all of the abuses simply because it combines all the forms of abuse—sexual, physical, emotional, verbal, and spiritual. But when someone is sexually abused by a church leader, another whole dimension of damage occurs. Being sexually abused by a church leader invalidates the victim's understanding of what the church is supposed to be, destroys all trust of the church and God, and misrepresents Christ and His love for the world.

Kinds of abuse by a pastor or church leader

A church leader can be abusive in many ways. We are most familiar with sexual, physical, emotional, and spiritual abuses.

However, there are other kinds of abuse within the context of the church. The list below provides a gamut of abuses that can be inflicted by a pastor or church leader.

- Child sexual abuse
- Adult sexual abuse
- Physical, emotional, and verbal abuse
- An emotional affair
- Spiritual abuse
- Abuse of power and boundary violations
- A breaching of confidential information
- False allegations, gossip, and slander
- Failure to use proper process
- Unethical behavior
- Illegal activity
- Fraud
- Defamation
- Clergy malpractice
- Invasion of privacy
- Undue influence

All of these can lead to legal action if the situations give evidence of wrongdoing and damage.

Child sexual abuse/adult sexual abuse by a church leader

When a pastor or church leader sexually touches, fondles, or in any other way is sexual to a minor, he commits child sexual abuse. This is a criminal activity and must be reported to the authorities. Sexual abuse by a church leader to a minor is a violation of law, and he can face fines and jail time if found guilty.

When a pastor or church leader sexually touches, fondles, or in any other way is sexual to another adult, including intercourse, he has sexually abused her, whether it was consensual or not. Because of the power in the position he holds as a church leader, any sexual activity with another, except for his wife, is sexual abuse. According to Fortune (1996) this goes beyond adultery, because there is not equal power between the two parties. The pastor holds the higher power and the victim has lesser power and fewer resources. Therefore, it is sexual abuse (p. 7).

Fortune (1996) asserts that sexual relations between a pastor and someone he serves or supervises is exploitive and abusive. First, it is a *violation of role*. This is not what the pastor was called to do. He was called by the church to serve in the best interests of others, not to satisfy his own needs. Second, it is a *misuse of authority and power*. He has more resources in the relationship and is the one responsible for keeping good boundaries to protect the congregant and himself. Third, it's about *taking advantage of the vulnerable*. Someone who seeks counsel from a pastor is vulnerable. She has fewer resources to draw from than the pastor does. The pastor must ensure protection of the vulnerable in his work with the counselee. Fourth, it's about *absence of meaningful consent*. Because there is an imbalance of power in the relationship, a victim's consent to sexual activity with the pastor does not excuse the pastor's responsibility to keep the relationship appropriate (p. 6–8).

Physical or emotional abuse by a church leader

Physical abuse is about doing physical harm to another. In the context of the church, it happens when a church leader purposely does physical harm to another. Anytime a church leader hits, punches, shoves, throws things, slaps, or otherwise hurts another person in the context of church leadership, physical abuse has occurred. Sometimes church leaders are known to verbally explode and rage. In their tirades, they may use ungodly language, throw things, or degrade others. A church leader may also use intimidation or threats to get others to listen to him. This is called verbal or emotional abuse.

Emotional affair

When a church leader and a congregant engage in long, intimate conversations about their personal affairs, desires, and wishes for one another, it's likely that an emotional affair has occurred. Kissing, touching each other, or intentionally meeting in certain places is further evidence that things have gone too far. Text messaging, e-mails, and voicemails not related to church activity reflect that the relationship has crossed the line and boundaries are being violated. Again, the church leader holds the responsibility in the relationship to keep conversations and interactions appropriate.

Spiritual Abuse

When Scripture is used to control, demean, ridicule, and shame someone, spiritual abuse has happened. When a pastor or church leader uses his position to get congregants to submit to his leadership, and he then uses that submission to have them do what he wants them to do, it is spiritual abuse.

Johnson and Van Vonderen (1991) speak about spiritual abuse. When a person is mistreated by a church leader in a way that the person feels spiritually disempowered, or when a church leader disregards another's emotions and spiritual well-being, spiritual abuse has happened (p. 20–21). Spiritually abusive church leaders are quick to silence anyone who challenges their authority, including shunning, isolating, or shaming them (p. 67). That approach by abusive leaders is their way of controlling their congregants with the intent to get them to come back to the church's control and authority.

Spiritually abusive pastors and church leaders distort the truth, lie, and accuse others. They lead with a lot of rules that protect the leaders and keep the power of the leadership intact. Should anyone confront that leadership, spiritually abusive leaders are quick to silence the matter, shun the complainant, and shove everything under the rug. Spiritually abusive leaders manipulate, control, and hide things.

Abuse of power and boundary violations

When a pastor or a church leader uses his position in the church to do what he wants, whether through manipulation or outright control, he crosses boundaries and has abused the power of his position. This kind of behavior is characterized by his working outside of what he is responsible for, and it is misuse and abuse of power.

Defining boundaries means determining where you need to say no and where you can say yes. If someone were to ask you how much money you make, by declining to answer that question, you are setting the boundary concerning what you want to disclose to another. If someone tells you that you are raising your children wrong and their way is better, that person is violating a boundary.

Boundary violations by a pastor or church leader may include the pastor making surprise drop-in visits when a woman is home alone, being intrusive in their congregants' private affairs, using excessive e-mailing or text messaging with congregants, sharing their own private information with congregants and others, getting involved in congregants' financial matters, or demonstrating favoritism toward certain congregants.

Healthy boundaries are crucial to a healthy church. Pastors and church leaders must work within their bounds of responsibility. Violations of boundaries in ministry occur when church leaders go outside their area of work and responsibility and involve themselves in things that are not their concern or responsibility. Poor boundaries intrude into the personal lives of others and involve trying to control, manipulate, or unduly influence others. This is abusive.

Breaching confidentiality

It's a big challenge for church leaders to respect and keep private the confidential information of their members and others. It's expected that when a congregant shares private information with a church leader, the shared information will remain confidential, unless it's life-threatening or the congregant has given permission to share it. Pastors, church councils, ministry staff, denominational personnel, and classis[1] leaders can be enticed to divulge the private information of others because it makes them feel powerful and significant. That kind of behavior is about getting the leaders' needs met and not about respecting the privacy of others. Breaching privileged and confidential communication and information is abusive and causes harm to innocent parties.

False allegations, gossip, and slander

Abuse by the church can occur when a leader spreads false allegations, gossip, or slander. Hearsay and gossip are a difficult problem in the Christian church. Spreading false allegations about others does great harm. Church leaders must remember to be focused on finding out truth before anything is said about another, and even then they must be careful about what is said. In the world of law, slander can lead to legal action. Titus 3:2 tells us, "Slander no one." Slandering others is a form of abuse.

Failure to use proper process

Church systems typically have many process and procedure policies to give direction as to how to deal with various matters of the church. However, in many churches, it's sometimes easier to avoid and ignore those procedures because of the time it takes to go through proper channels when an issue needs to

1   Classis is a governing body of elders or pastors in some Reformed churches.

be addressed. This causes pastors and church leaders to act on their own without following the established guidelines of the church.

There is a reason for establishing guidelines and procedures when addressing grievances in the church. Although these guidelines are just that—guidelines—they were established and adopted with the understanding that their use would provide protection for the complainant and the accused. Failure to follow established guidelines increases the likelihood that more harm will occur to the involved parties and church members. Time is typically a problem with the use of procedures. Councils and elder boards need reminders that completing grievance or appeal processes in a timely manner ensures better outcomes for all. Failure to follow policies and procedures is abusive and does harm to the involved parties.

Unethical behavior

Behavior that does not reflect proper conduct for a particular position or expectation is called unethical. If your doctor was drunk when you had an appointment with him, his behavior would be considered unethical. When the conduct and behavior of pastors and church leaders does not reflect what you would consider proper for their offices, it is unethical. For example, it is unethical for a pastor to counsel congregants when the congregants' issues are outside the pastor's training and education. It is unethical for council members to make fun of and ridicule congregants of different color or race or for them to make rude or crude jokes about church members.

In addressing the subject of abuse, it would be considered unethical and abusive for a pastor to kiss a woman, to flirt with someone, to hug excessively, or to send e-mails that talk about sex. This would be using his position as pastor to meet his needs.

Illegal activity

One might not think a pastor would get involved in illegal activity, but it happens. Illegal activity can be something as seemingly minor as failing to cite his sources when writing sermons or as major as stealing from church accounts to pay bills. Examples of illegal activity by a pastor or church leader include getting involved in scams, sharing pornographic materials with minors, and sexually abusing children.

Fraud

Taylor (1990) explains fraud as "deceitful acts for unlawful gain" (p.26). In the context of church leadership, fraud would be the church leader using his position of authority to illegally gain something for himself or others. As Christians, we believe that we must be honest and that God requires honesty in our dealings with others and in the business world. So when a pastor or church leader intentionally deceives others for gain, fraud has occurred. The church leader has also abused the power of his position by wronging others to get what he wants.

Defamation

Taylor (1996) defines defamation as the damaging of a person's reputation, character, or occupation through words or publication (p.41). Defamation goes beyond slander in that it includes verbal and/or written false information about someone else which damages the person. Defamation happens when a mass e-mail is sent out degrading and falsely accusing another person, or when false information about a person is posted on Facebook and that information is open for anyone to read. If that information causes damage to the person's reputation, defamation is likely to have occurred.

In the context of the church, pastors and church leaders are not to defame anyone. As Christians, if we make public false information about another, we are disobeying the command to "encourage one another and build each other up" (I Thessalonians 5:11, NIV Study Bible). Defamation is a form of abuse and abuse of a leader's position in the church.

Clergy malpractice

Clergy malpractice is when clergy use negligent counseling practices and cause injury. Therapists, doctors, attorneys, and others must follow certain standards in their work as professionals. Because pastors are unlicensed and do not hold to a certain professional standard, it remains unclear what actions or behaviors are considered below a pastor's level of required care (Taylor, 1999, p. 108–9).

When a pastor's care is considered below the required level of competence of other clergy and the counselee suffers injury, clergy malpractice is likely. When there are no set standards for pastors to follow, determining whether a pastor's actions can be considered negligent is something courts will need to decide (Taylor, 1996 p. 110–1).

Here are a few challenges pastors may face when the question of clergy malpractice surfaces. A pastor becomes aware that his counselee intends to commit suicide. Since there is no contract and typically no charge for his services, is the pastor required by law to report? If he reports, could it be considered a breach of confidentiality? Another challenge for a pastor might be discovering that his counselee has intent to harm or kill someone. Is an unlicensed pastor required to fulfill the duty to warn? Either choice could cause litigation for the pastor.

The abuse of his position comes when he is reckless and neglectful during a time he needs to be careful in his response. When he ignores a person's threat to harm him- or herself or others and does not consider carefully what the best course of action is, he neglects his office as pastor or church leader. In cases like this, documentation must show that the pastor was very careful about how he responded to the situation and that his consultation with other professionals reflects a responsible response to the situation.

Invasions of privacy

Once trust has been built between a congregant and a pastor, the congregant comes to believe that he or she can share private information with the pastor and the pastor will hold that information in confidence. When trust has been established, the congregant will begin to seek out help from the pastor. A pastor's ability to develop trust with his congregants is key to effective ministry (Taylor, 1996 p. 120).

According to Taylor, if a minister is accused of invading someone's privacy, it is viewed by most as a serious breach of the minister's moral, and sometimes legal obligation to that person. Such accusations shock our consciences, because we believe that protecting, not exploiting another's privacy, is the very job of those in ministry (p. 120).

Examples of possible acts which could constitute invasion of privacy are:

- A pastor appoints himself to be an investigator to determine if one of his congregants is having an affair.
- A pastor makes private facts and information about another public without the person's knowledge or consent.
- A pastor presents publicly false and skewed information about another, which causes damage to the congregant.
- A pastor uses someone's name or picture publically without regard or respect for the person and without proper consent or knowledge to do so.

(Taylor, 1996, p. 121–9)

It would be abusive for a pastor to involve himself in matters outside of his bounds and/or present information about another without proper permission. It is crucial for pastors to build and maintain trust with those in their care. Keeping information private and confidential is critical in doing that.

Undue influence

Undue influence involves exploiting a person by taking unfair and illegal advantage. Whereas fraud concerns are about not being forthright about a transaction, undue influence is more about using the weaknesses or deficiencies of another for gain. In situations of undue influence, one of the parties is usually in a superior position to the other. For pastors, issues of undue influence arise when an elderly, ill, or impaired person agrees to give large sums of money to a pastor. It can be alleged that the pastor, who is superior in the relationship, somehow persuaded the individual to give the money, thereby taking advantage of someone who is weaker or more vulnerable (Taylor, 1996, pp. 135–6). This is abusive.

Conclusion

Abuse by the church happens in many ways. Only through careful work and a church leader's willingness to work on his self-awareness will issues of abuse and the misuse of power in ministry be reduced. Issues of arrogance, narcissism, and entitlement by the church leader are central to the occurrence of abuse and misuse of the ministry office. When pastors and church leaders are more concerned with serving themselves than they are about serving others, their approach to ministry takes the downward spiral of abusing others.

Although sexual abuse by clergy is the most damaging and horrendous of all the abuses, abuse in a broader sense is also what brings harm to people and mars the name of Christ. As you and your church leaders continue to weigh how your leadership works, focus on whether the approach used is controlling, rigid, self-seeking, and arrogant or if it is more about carelessness, recklessness and an approach that lacks accountability. If so, it's likely your church leadership is abusing those near you.

Chapter 5
Stories of Abuse and Its Effects:
In the Christian Environment

This is what the Sovereign Lord says: Woe to the shepherds of Israel who only take care of themselves! You have not strengthened the weak or healed the sick or bound up the injured. You have not brought back the strays or searched for the lost. You have ruled them harshly and brutally. I am against the shepherds and will hold them accountable.

—Ezekiel 34: 2–4, 10

Story One

The church is located in a small Iowa town. Its beginnings were about a people who desired a more conservative approach to the interpretation of the Bible, worship style, and the importance of male headship. The church grew rather quickly, and the members' search for a conservative pastor to fit their style of leadership and teachings soon saw success. Or so they thought (Winters, 2011).

Several years passed when suddenly the pastor resigned

abruptly. Abuse allegations had been brought to the church's council, and when he was confronted by the church leaders, the pastor resigned and he and his family quickly left town (Winters, 2011).

As news reports came forward, the community was shocked and angered about what the pastor had done. He was accused of raping several women in his study, threatening them if they should tell, and using his role as a pastor to get his own needs met; these reports saddened the people of his church and community (Winters, 2011). Rumors spread about who the victims were and what would happen next. Confusion set in about what had happened. Questions surfaced. Was this adultery? Sexual abuse? Rape? What if it was consensual?

What happened between the pastor and these women was more than adultery. Much more. This was sexual abuse. This was abuse of power. This was taking advantage of women who were vulnerable and seeking help from someone they thought they could trust. This was about betrayal. This was about a pastor taking care of his own needs at the expense of others' well-being (Fortune 1996, p. 7). And in this case, it was rape.

What happened between the pastor and these women is about spiritual abuse. A pastor, who represents Christ and his church and who is mandated to care for the spiritual needs of God's people, abuses a sacred office to have his sexual and emotional needs met. Using lying, deception, and cunning, the pastor convinced these women and the people of his church that he was a man of God. But his dark side showed what he really was: abusive, controlling, manipulative, and evil.

Benyei et al. tell us in *When a Congregation Is Betrayed* that pastors have a fiduciary relationship and responsibility to their congregations (p.21). What does this mean? It means that because of the pastor's position, he has the responsibility to hold sacred trust in the relationship with his congregants. When he takes the position as pastor, he makes an agreement with the entire congregation that he is responsible for conducting himself in an appropriate manner in his relationships with the church members and in any interactions outside the church. When he breaks that trust by violating a member of the congregation or someone outside the church membership, trust between him and the church, and between him and the entire congregation, is broken. Therefore, because it is his fiduciary duty to maintain appropriate boundaries in relationships with his congregation and community, he—not the victim—is at fault for the wrong that occurred.

Marie Fortune says, "I define clergy sexual abuse in the following way: Clergy sexual misconduct occurs whenever a member of the clergy engages in sexual behaviors with someone for whom he or she has spiritual responsibility" (p.47).

Spiritual responsibility is about caring for and attending to the spiritual well-being of others. Spiritual responsibility is about doing what is best for those the pastor is entrusted with. By doing all he can to help his congregants and others grow in Christ and to love Him more, the pastor fulfills his mandate of being a healing agent in God's broken world. But when abuse happens, the pastor neglects his call to care for the spiritual well-being of others. He instead destroys.

When the pastor turns from that mandate and uses others to meet his needs, when he exploits those who are vulnerable and uses deception and power to disillusion them, when he threatens and uses coercion to control and dominate, abuse occurs.

Effects of adult sexual abuse by a church leader

We have already seen the effects of sexual abuse of one adult by another adult. Adult sexual abuse causes extensive damage to the victim, including problems with anxiety, depression, post-traumatic stress syndrome (PTSD), sleepless nights, fears of not being safe, fears of intimacy, and much more. As these effects take their toll on victims of sexual abuse, abuse by a church leader increases the damage all the more. Now not only does the victim have to deal with the normal issues of sexual abuse, she also has to deal with the fact that it was done by a church leader.

We grew up believing that pastors and church leaders were safe people. We trusted them. We grew up believing they were men of God and they cared about us. We were taught to obey them and to entrust our spiritual lives to them. We take them at their word and trust that they know best when problems arise. We want to be a flock that follows our shepherd, and we expend much energy to show our dedication to helping and supporting our churches and our pastors.

But when sexual abuse by a church leader occurs, everything changes. When it becomes known to us that a church leader had sexual contact with someone other than his wife, we are shocked. Our thinking becomes frozen. Our minds cannot process it. What we came to believe about church leaders now crashes to the ground. We question how this could happen. We wonder if it is true. We fight within ourselves. One part says: *This can't be true. He would never do that; he's a pastor.* Another part questions why someone would lie about it. We go back and forth, doubting ourselves. Did we miss something here? Don't we know what we're doing? Are we naïve?

And the frustration continues. How can someone who is trained in understanding Scripture, who preaches sermons every Sunday, and who is trusted to be an effective leader have sex with someone who is not his wife? How can a pastor molest, fondle, or perform sex acts with someone for whom he has spiritual responsibility? How can someone betray a sacred trust? How can the abuser justify his behavior when he clearly knows what the Bible teaches about such sins? A battle rages within us as we try to understand this.

Primary victim

The abused woman is the primary victim. She carries the heaviest part of this burden. The woman now has more problems than she had before she sought help from the pastor. Her ability to trust, love, and engage in fellowship with the church is ruined. She doesn't want to go to church anymore. She feels unsafe and unprotected. She has triggers that set off anxiety and panic attacks. She worries that she will see him in the community. She fears that others will find out what happened. She blames herself for what he did to her, and the shame she feels is more than she can bear. She isolates herself in the midst of it all and cuts herself off from family and community.

Her understanding of the church is confused. A place she loved has become a place of hurt and contradictions. Her community of faith is now a place of violence, turmoil, and anger. When she tries to explain how she feels about church, people tell her to forget it and move on. They tell her to quit making such a big deal of it and to just "forgive." At night she can't shut off her thinking. She ruminates about the events of the abuse and the conversations that happened in connection to the abuse, and she weeps and mourns over what happened.

Going to church is no longer peaceful. She can't sit through a service because she can't stop thinking and crying about what the leadership did to her. As she sits in the pew she sees all of the things that represent church— the cross, the denominational symbols, the Bible references, and the pulpit—and she goes into a panic attack. All that stands for God, the Bible, and her faith has been torn to shreds, and she weeps over her great loss. Her place of worship has become a place of war and causes her anguish.

Her marriage and family life suffer. She struggles with being intimate with her husband. She finds herself not trusting anyone or not knowing whom to trust. Her ability to do her day-to-day activities diminishes. Her concentration and focus are shattered. She is impatient with her family, and she finds herself crying uncontrollably. She is angry at those around her, and she lashes out at them. At other times, she hides in her bedroom and refuses to face her family or the world. Her soul suffers.

She is angry at God. She wonders why God didn't protect her and save her. She thought God would bring good into her life, not evil. So why would He let this happen? What good can come from being sexually abused by a pastor?

Her idea of church is changed. What she thought was true about church is destroyed. What she was taught by her parents about church when she was growing up is shattered. Her belief that we should obey leadership because they always know best is now a lie to her. While sitting in church, everything she sees no longer holds meaning. The church and what it stands for is a joke to her now. And it is impossible to concentrate on worshiping God when all her mind can think about is her abuse experience with a church leader.

Secondary victims

Her family, council members, and the church members, who are the secondary victims, are horrified at what has happened. As the details become known to them, they feel their own sense of betrayal by the church leader. They question why he would do such a thing, and they ask themselves if they should have seen it coming. They think back to times when they worked well with the church leader, and they wonder how they could have been fooled by the church leader's motives and approaches. Some will have feelings of confusion, anger, and shock while others will turn to denying the truth and saying it never happened.

Betrayal of trust by a church leader is no small thing. When councils and congregations call a pastor, they assume that the pastor or church leader will be trustworthy. They grew up believing that pastors and church leaders were good people. They were taught to trust clergy and pastors and were taught to believe that those who graduate from seminaries are competent at leading a church appropriately and responsibly. When a pastor betrays that trust, all are affected.

There are many responses by church leaders and church members when a church leader sexually abuses someone. The secondary victims will feel hurt and betrayed. Some will protect the pastor and say he didn't mean anything by it. Some won't understand what all of the fuss is about. Some will blame the victim and say she seduced him. Some will refuse to get involved because it might ruin their names or reputations. Some will leave the church. And the anger of some will make going to the grocery store a horrifying experience. I have seen all of these things happen in churches where the pastor abused.

Secondary victims will need to deal with their anger, frustration, and confusion with what happened and determine how to respond to the pastor. They will also find themselves ruminating about what happened, facing sleepless nights, needing a place to process emotion, and weeping that such a thing could happen in their church. Secondary victims will be forced to wake up and realize that abuse by a church leader is real and that their church is not immune to the things like this. Secondary victims will need to learn about this subject and will need to search out answers about how to respond to this kind of a problem in the church. Their naïveté will diminish as they learn about violations of boundaries, power and control issues, and betrayal of trust when a pastor abuses.

Story Two

When Wesley was in his early teen years, he joined his church's youth club for boys. This was a Christian club where boys from ages ten to fourteen learned about camping, what it means to be a good citizen, and what it means to be a Christian young man.

After he belonged to this club for about two years, Wesley told his mom he didn't want to go anymore. He didn't give her any specific reason why; he just didn't want to. A short time later, one of the leaders of the club was asked to resign. No one was told why; they were told only that the boys of the club were told by the elders "to forgive and move on."

Now in his mid-forties, Wesley finds himself extremely depressed and anxious. For years, he has gone from therapy group to therapy group, trying to understand why he feels so depressed and anxious. His marriage broke up a few years ago, and a short time later he realized he could no longer maintain full-time employment. With no marriage and no ability to keep a job, he moved to Michigan to live in his mom's basement. Now he was again in a depression group, trying to understand what was wrong with him.

Then one day it happened. While in group, he asked the leader if it was possible for someone who was abused as a child to still be affected by that abuse. The answer was yes. For him, it was like a light came on. His journey for answers began.

He started by trying to remember what happened to him in his childhood church. He remembered the elders telling the boys' club to "forgive and move on" at one of the evening church services. He remembered not wanting to go the boys' club anymore. He remembered camping trips with a man named Al. He asked his brother if he remembered anything. His brother shared with him that there was a time when he, Al, and Wesley were in a car together, and Al kissed Wesley and forced him to touch him.

The pieces were starting to come together.

Wesley wanted to know more. He contacted his childhood church and told the pastor that he was remembering abuse that had happened at that church. He shared some of what he had already uncovered. But the pastor was not engaged, and the pastor's response was a great disappointment. "You wouldn't want to bring all this up and hurt these people now, would you? We live in a broken world. You need to accept that."

But that didn't stop Wesley. He persevered. He contacted some of the other leaders of that church. They confirmed that what he was saying was true. There was a man named Al who had sexually abused the boys of the boys club in the early 1970s. There were many other victims besides him. Al was asked to resign when a parent reported the abuse to the council. He was told that most of the abuse was done on camping trips to the mountains. The abuse included sodomy, fondling, and sex acts. It was true that the council had told the boys at a Sunday evening service to "forgive and move on." There was no call to child protective services, no investigations by the council, and no reporting to the parents what had happened.

He was starting to connect himself to who he was, what his childhood was about, and why he was the way he was today.

Effects of childhood sexual abuse by a church leader

Wesley said that he had never been able to connect to his emotions. It was as if his emotions as an adult were still at the place they'd been in when he was abused. Managing adult problems and issues with the emotions of a thirteen-year-old does not work. He shared that it was as if life and emotions could not come together. In his marriage, he couldn't connect to his wife—he couldn't feel what she was feeling and he couldn't feel what he was feeling. His disconnect with his feelings made his adult life, including his marriage, a very hard thing for him.

He suffered from several health issues related to his childhood abuse. One of them was severe diabetes. During the time of addressing his abuse to the church leaders, records show that his glucose level would spike to 500 mg/dL (normal is less than 140). His eyes had light sensitivity and he often could not be up before 3:00 p.m. because his eyes could not tolerate the brightness of daylight. He had skin breakouts on his arms. When he showed his arms at the hearing when he presented his case to church leaders, the delegates at the meeting were shocked and aggrieved at what they saw.

Wesley could no longer work. Although he had been fully

employed for many years, eventually his depression and anxiety took over and he could no longer do it. He told of his exhaustion and fatigue, his despair and sadness, and his confusion about what had happened to him. He said that his life was over and there wasn't anything left to live for. Everything looked hopeless for him, and it took all his energy just to get out of bed and accomplish something for the day.

He didn't want much to do with church anymore. He believed that things about God didn't make sense. What he had learned about God and God's love as a child was hard to believe. Because the church had done such bad things to him, it was hard for him to embrace anything that dealt with church. When coming into the sanctuary of the church where the hearing for his case was held, he couldn't process it. He kept on saying, "What does this really mean, 'Do this in remembrance of me'?" Tying this and other symbols and verses related to God or the church caused confusion and hurt.

A church leader chose to ruin this man's life. A church leader was more concerned about meeting his deviant sexual needs than about empowering a young man to grow and mature in a Christ-like way. A church leader refused to obey what the Bible teaches and instead took advantage of a vulnerable young man. The result was a man deeply hurt by the church.

Story three

In the 1980s and the 1990s, missionary children who attended the New Tribes Mission School (NTM) in the village of Fanda in Senegal, Africa, were abused. Children placed in that school experienced sexual, physical, emotional, and spiritual abuse. The treatment they received there was criminal (*GRACE Report*, 2010, p. 1).

After an unsuccessful attempt in 1997 to investigate what happened there, the leadership of the Fanda school hired an outside source to investigate the abuse during those two decades. The outside investigative team called GRACE (Godly

Response to Abuse in the Christian Environment) was hired to investigate what the teachers and boarding staff did to the children at the school (p. 3).

The report states that twenty-two to twenty-seven students reported sexual abuse by the staff, more than thirty-five students experienced physical and emotional abuse by the staff, and everyone who attended the school experienced spiritual abuse (p. 14–15).

Victims of abuse at the Fanda school share their stories in the report. Four victims tell stories of the staff sneaking around at night and lying in girls' beds, fondling them and teaching them about masturbation (p.12). Two victims said that excessive force was used when they were being punished. One was forced to eat her own vomit. Another victim's arm was broken when she was yanked out of class (p. 16). Four victims told how a staff member kissed them on their lips, held them down and licked their ears, and fondled his wife's breast in front of the kids (p. 13).

One man in particular repeatedly abused the young girls of the school. He invited the little girls to sleepovers and would creep into their rooms at night to caress, fondle, and kiss them. He rubbed his body against theirs, digitally manipulated their genitals, taught them how to masturbate, and played shower games with them. He told them that bad things would happen if they told anyone and said that no one would believe them. He told the girls about his close walk with the Lord while he was sexually abusing them (p. 18–19). The children were warned that if they ever told anyone, their parents would be distracted from their work and Africans would go to hell because of them (p. 10 of GRACE report).

Effects of childhood abuse in the Christian environment

Having experienced sexual, physical, emotional, and spiritual abuse, the Fanda victims share the effects of their abuse experiences. They are plagued with memory loss, depression, guilt, feelings of powerlessness, experiencing panic attacks, and the inability to sing in church. Anger, fear, distrust of adults, suicidal ideation and attempts, self-harm, eating disorders, and substance abuse were reported, as were sexual confusion and repression, the desire to run away, joining the occult, and being involved in criminal behavior. Some victims have been imprisoned (p. 25–26).

The spiritual abuse of the Fanda children was extensive. Some of the comments from victims in the *GRACE Report* include:

> "Because of NTM, I absolutely *despise* anybody who calls themselves [*sic*] a Christian."

> "The spiritual abuse came in the form of twisted theology. The theology seemed to say, 'God is waiting for you to screw up and when you do, He will punish you.' God was always angry … The philosophy was that the kids had to listen to the adults because God talks through adults."

> "[I]… have no desire to share the gospel. [My] … experience with Fanda has destroyed any spirituality that I had with Christianity. [I]… would like to have something to share with [my]…children besides Santa Claus…[I] hope [I] … will understand God one day."

> "[She] hated God or at least who she knew Him to be. For years she pushed Him away…[S]he began going to a Baptists church and the pastor preached about anger one day. That night she cried all night about her anger and she wondered how to get un-angry. She knew she had to let go of her anger for the sake of herself and for her family. By morning she was broken and everything changed since then."

(p. 24–25)

Conclusion

The effects of sexual, physical, emotional, and spiritual abuse are devastating and horrific. Whether it is an adult or child who is abused, the effects linger longer than anyone of us want to admit or realize. Although we desire the pain, the memories, and the emotional upheaval to go away, desire alone is not enough. Recovery can last a lifetime and when it happens in the context of the Christian environment, the healing is even more difficult and painful.

Chapter 6
More Stories of Abuse in the Church

From the least to the greatest, all are greedy for gain. Prophets and priests alike all practice deceit. They dress the wound of my people as though it were not serious. 'Peace, peace,' they say, when there is no peace. Are they ashamed of their loathsome conduct? No, they have no shame at all; they do not even know how to blush.

—Jer. 6:13–14

Outside of sexual, physical, emotional, and spiritual abuse, the church can abuse in other ways. These "lesser" kinds of abuse can do extensive damage and harm, and in some cases, legal action may be used against the church leader and the church.

Lesser kinds of abuse by the church include: emotional affairs, abusing power and violating boundaries, revealing the confidential information of another, false allegations, gossiping and slandering another, failing to use the proper process, using unethical behavior, engaging in illegal activity, fraud, defamation, clergy malpractice, invading a person's privacy, and using undue influence.

More stories of church abuse

1. A pastor became emotionally involved with one of his parishioners. This woman, who was abused as a child, was a member of a regional church committee. When decisions made by the committee were not to this woman's liking, she began to make regular contact with her pastor to complain to him about the committee chair. The complaints, which were outside of the domain of the pastor's work, involve the woman's perception of unfair treatment by the committee chair. Through her own deception and distortions, she managed to convince the pastor that she was right and the chairperson was doing wrong.

   Having been duped by the woman's lies and distortions, the pastor crossed boundary lines and decided to take the matter into his own hands. Without any contact with the committee chair, he wrote a four-page letter to the chair accusing her of doing things she had never done. On the top of each page was a warning that she was never to tell anyone about this letter. Along with that, he sent a threatening e-mail to her, again warning her not to tell anyone about the letter.

   After contacting an attorney, the chairperson turned the letter over to church authorities. They were appalled at what the pastor had done and they confronted him. The pastor had abused his position of authority by becoming emotionally involved with a parishioner, violating boundaries, and falsely accusing the chairperson.

2. A respected leader in a non-profit agency was loved by his board, his employees, and the shareholders of the non-profit. One of his female employees left

after being asked to secure outside counseling, and a church fact-finding panel called and confronted the leader about allegations of abuse. Later it was discovered that the allegations were instigated by a pastor who was emotionally involved with the woman and came to believe her allegations to be true.

The fact-finding panel neglected to follow proper process. Without knowledge or permission from the governing council, the panel met with the woman. As the panel continued their work, it was found that the allegations did not fit the criteria for an investigation. However, the panel members continued the investigation, egged on by the involved pastor, who was pushing for a report.

When the governing officials learned what the fact-finding panel was doing, they told the panel to stop their work immediately. They didn't. The panel refused to listen to the governing officials and sent out a report of what the woman said anyway. The report defamed the man's name and reputation, although the governing officials and his attorney's representatives cleared him of any wrongdoing.

When the governing officials came to know that the panel had ignored their directives, the governing officials scrambled to retrieve the inappropriate letters, but two letters were never retrieved. The panel and the pastor used unethical behavior, failed to use proper process, defamed, slandered, gossiped, and abused power.

3. She worked in a high position within the church structure. She had a background in mental health education and training, and a part of her job was to ensure safety policies and procedures in the workplace. After completing service for one of the

victims her office served, she called a church leader and told him private and confidential information about the victim without obtaining proper consent.

Later, when the victim was told by the church leader what the woman had done, the victim reported the incident to the woman's governing authorities. Her governing board refused to address the issue and instead called her breach of confidential information "pastoral care." She had abused the victim by revealing private and confidential information. She had misused her power, engaged in unethical behavior, and violated boundaries.

4. She changed churches because her church supported her husband's abusive approach toward her. When she came to the new church and told the leaders the abuse she was experiencing in her marriage, they told her to "reconcile." They informed her that "anything is possible with God" and "God hates divorce."

    Greatly distressed about this, she told a member of the congregation what was going on. When the concerned member confronted the elder board, again they said that anything is possible with God. The concerned member clearly spelled out why supporting a husband's abusive behavior was unacceptable and wrong. Later they apologized to the woman. The elder board was ignorant about how to handle issues of domestic violence and their response was emotionally abusive, a misuse of power, and negligence of office.

5. He brought his childhood sexual abuse case by a church leader through the proper process within the church system. When his case came to the top governing authorities, it was ruled that his

case would not be heard because it did not fit their criteria for hearing cases. Feeling deeply hurt by the church again, he talked to the senior leader of the denomination a few days later. The church leader was irritated about having this man in his office, and he told the man nothing else could be done and asked him to leave his office. That night, when he told his advocate about what had happened, his distress and hurt ran deep. He had been kicked out of the office of the senior church leader. He was abused by the church as a child and re-abused when he tried to tell his story to the church today. The church leaders abused their power, and the senior church leader abused power and showed unethical behavior.

6. A pastor took online sermons and preached them without citing the author. When confronted, he denied it, until someone revealed his lies by showing the original text he had copied. At first he admitted that he had taken this shortcut a few times. As time went along, it was found that he had done it hundreds of times. The pastor was unethical, abused power, and engaged in illegal activity.

7. A pastor was involved in online gambling. He became addicted and soon was unable to pay what he owed. When his credit cards were maxed out and he had no money to pay his bills, he took money from some of the church accounts. When confronted about the missing funds, he admitted he had taken some of the church's money to cover his gambling debts. The pastor abused his position, violated boundaries, engaged in unethical behavior, and engaged in illegal activity.

8. A man from the congregation met with his pastor and shared with his pastor that he thought that

his wife was having an affair. As the husband and pastor discussed the matter, they made plans to follow her when she left work.

Several weeks later, they carried out their plan. As they followed her, she traveled for some time and then pulled over in front of a small bar. They observed her parking the car and being greeted by a man who kissed her. The two of them went into the bar. The pastor had violated boundaries, behaved unethically, and invaded the privacy of one of his members.

9. A pastor visited an elderly woman weekly as she was nearing the end of her life. He knew his charm easily influenced her and she often told him she loved his visits. Realizing the pastor had large unpaid medical bills because of a handicapped child, the elderly woman offered to leave some of her money to the pastor. The pastor, relieved to hear that some of the medical burden could be lifted, carefully asked her if she was sure that she wanted to do this. She was sure.

    A short time later the pastor received a sizeable check from the elderly woman. The pastor quickly cashed the check and paid the medical bills. When this became known to family members, they alleged that the pastor had done wrong. In this case, the pastor had abused his power, violated boundaries, and used undue influence.

10. When he was a child, the man had been sexually abused by a church leader. When he confronted church officials as an adult, a church hearing regarding what had happened was planned.

    As the advocate for the abused explained what had happened to the man as a boy and now charged the current church leaders with negligence for not responding properly to his allegations, the presiding officer (who was one of the pastors of that region) of the hearing made fun of the advocate and victim during their presentation. Rolling his eyes, distractingly tapping his pen, and smirking about what was being said, the presiding officer showed himself to be inappropriate and subjective about the case. However, in the denomination's governing manual it clearly states that the presiding officer should remain neutral during the proceedings.

When the church leaders came forward to present their side of things, again he was subjective. He looked at the church officials, nodded approvingly at what was being said, and smiled at the church officials as if saying the church leaders were right again.

The presiding officer failed to use proper process, was unethical, abused power, had poor boundaries, and was emotionally abusive.

Chapter 7
Forgiving: What the Church Should Do
(And What If the Church Doesn't)

Therefore, strengthen your feeble arms and weak knees. Make level paths for your feet, so that the [abused] may not be disabled, but rather healed.

—Hebrews 12:12–13

How does one forgive the church? How does one forgive someone who knows it is wrong to use and abuse others but does it anyway? How does one forgive someone who is an authority on Scripture and biblical teaching but abuses? How does one forgive an institution or an organization that represents the name of Christ when it has abused? How does one engage back into church functions and worship when hurt, anger, and anxiety dominate every thought about the church? What must the church do to help make it possible for the victim to forgive the church?

Pastors and church leaders have fiduciary responsibility for the people they serve. Remember that fiduciary responsibility means that church leaders have the responsibility to keep relationships between themselves and others appropriate (Benyei et al., 2006, p. 21). It is not unreasonable to think that pastors and church leaders should be trusted people. Trusting pastors and church leaders is core to ministry and building the Church of God. When we trust, we build one another up and build up our faith communities.

That is why when a pastor breaks this sacred trust by abusing others it is so hard to forgive. All that we learned from our childhood about pastors and church, all that we came to believe to be true about church and its leadership, and all that we thought to be true about churches crashes when the pastor abuses.

Approximate Justice-Making

What should the church do in order to help make it possible for the victim to forgive the church? Fortune (1996) suggests seven elements of approximate justice-making that must be present when abuse allegations come forward against a church leader. These justice-making elements are a part of what the victim needs to help her with the healing, recovery, and forgiveness process.

The seven elements of justice-making are truth-telling, acknowledgement, compassion, protection of the vulnerable, accountability for the abuser, restitution, and vindication (Fortune, 1996, p. 9–10). Let's look at each one.

1. Truth-telling (p. 9). The church leaders must get to the truth of what happened. This is the most important part of the investigative process and the hardest to do. When wrong has occurred, often the involved parties struggle to tell the truth. There are distortions and skewed perceptions; there are lies and confusion. However, it is crucial that the church leaders get at the truth.
2. Acknowledgment (p. 9). Acknowledgment means that the governing authorities listen to the victim's

story and believe her. The council says to the victim, "We hear what you said. We believe you. We are angry that this happened to you. We are grieved that this man did this to you."

3. Compassion (p. 9). The leaders must show compassion towards the victim, her family, and others significantly affected by the abuse. This means that the church leaders are willing to suffer with the victim, show they are empathic about the situation, and grieve with those directly involved.

4. Protection of the vulnerable (p. 9). Church leaders must do all they can to make sure this never happens again to anyone. They will take all of the safety precautions necessary regarding relationships between church leaders and congregants, they will write child safety and congregant safety policies for the church, and they will invite trainers to lead workshops for the congregation to explain what abuse in the church looks like. The elder board will reinforce their safety policies by visiting regularly with church leaders to ensure that they are practicing safety in their counseling setting, instructional settings, and childcare programs. When church leaders protect the vulnerable, they actively ensure that abuse will never happen again at the church.

5. Accountability of the abuser (p. 10). Holding the abuser accountable for what happened means that the governing board or council will confront the abuser, ask questions, and require answers to those questions. Accountability is when the elders bring the allegations to the abuser and expect nothing less than the truth.

6. Restitution (p. 10). Restitution is payback to the victim for the pain she experience because of the abuse. Restitution in our society means money.

Paying for the victim's counseling and therapy expenses, medical expenses, and time away from work to address the abuse issues is restitution.

7. Vindication (p. 10). Vindication is relief. Vindication is when the church relieves the victim of the pain she endured because of the abuse. It's a way for the church to lift the burden of what she had to bear.

Using these seven elements of justice-making when responding to abuse allegations in the context of the church will give to the victim what she needs while she works through the forgiveness process.

Acts of Repentance

Fortune (1996, p.12) also talks about acts of repentance when allegations of abuse surface. When the church engages in these four acts of repentance, the forgiveness process for the victim can begin. In order for the victim to begin the process of forgiving the pastor and the church, the church must pay restitution, relinquish power, acknowledge the reality of the abuse, and take responsibility for the abuse.

1. Restitution (p. 12). The victim must have payment for the damage and harm that was done to her. This payment can be in the form of financial assistance to cover counseling and therapy as well as medical bills. In the legal system, restitution is the money paid out in a civil suit.

2. Relinquishment of power (p. 12). Relinquishment of power is taking away the power the abuser has. In the case of a pastor, it means that his preaching license is taken away, he is no longer allowed to preach or lead worship services, he resigns from all leadership positions for church committees or groups, and he is forced to resign from any other office that he holds in connection with the church.

3. Acknowledgement of the reality of the abuse (p. 12). Not only does the church take a strong stand against the abuse that has happened and make the stand clear and public to the congregation, the pastor as well must acknowledge to the abuser and the congregation the wrong he has done.

4. Taking responsibility for the abuse (p.12). The church and the pastor must take responsibility for what happened. The pastor will admit what he did, say that it was wrong, and take responsibility for it. Any harm or hurt he caused is his responsibility and he owns the blame. The leadership as well will take the blame and fault for what happened. They will admit to any negligence in supervising they were guilty of.

The victim should be assured that she has been heard by the church authorities, that the church has taken action to address the abuse, and that it has done all in its power to bring justice to the victim.

The 3 A's and the 3 R's

One way for church leaders to approach helping a victim abused by a church leader is to use the 3 A's and the 3 R's approach. The three A's are accountability, acknowledgment, and apology. The 3 R's are restitution, relinquishment of power, and relief.

Accountability (Fortune, 1996, p. 10) is realized when church leaders go to the abuser and demand answers to their questions. They should expect honesty and truthfulness from the pastor and should investigate fully the details of what happened. Acknowledgment (Fortune, 1996, p. 10) is when the church leaders admit that the abuse has happened, tell what they know to the congregants using proper limits and boundaries, and verbalize the wrongness of what has happened: "We have investigated this and it is true. We are greatly aggrieved that this has happened." With <u>apology</u>, the abuser and the church leaders tell the victim and her family how sorry they are that this happened. The pastor says, "I am deeply sorry for what I did. It was wrong. I sinned against you. I apologize." The council says, "We as church leaders are sorry that we did this to you. We take responsibility for not supervising our pastor better. We apologize."

<u>Restitution</u> comes to the victim. It is payment to the victim to try to right the wrong that was done. It's not that it will make everything right, but it will help give the victim feel that she has been given some measure of justice for the wrong that was done to her (or him). <u>Relinquishment</u> of power is the pastor being directed to step down from his position as pastor and any other church leadership position he has. This forced step down makes the power between the victim and the abuser more equal. With him out of his position of power, it is possible for the victim to forgive. When allegations of abuse by a church leader are addressed, well and thoroughly, <u>relief</u> (or vindication) is felt by the victim. This feeling of relief comes from knowing that she was heard by the church leaders, that the church authorities took it seriously, and that they did something about it (Fortune, 1996, p. 12).

Other ways the church can enhance the forgiveness process for the victim

When the victim comes forward to present her[2] allegations of abuse by a church leader, the governing board of the church must take several immediate actions. The church council or

---

2   We have mostly been talking about abuse by a male pastor or church leader of a female victim, so, for the sake of simplicity, we will use the female pronouns when talking about the victim and male pronouns to discuss the abuser. However, as we know in the case of the Roman Catholic Church, males can be victims as well. These guidelines apply equally to male and female victims and male and female accusers.

governing board should engage in a fact-finding/investigative process. If the charges are weighty and probable, appointing and using an investigative committee or an abuse response team is necessary to collect information, determine likelihood, and provide a letter of facts and recommendations to the council/ elder board about the case. Depending on the church structure, the council or elder board will give a direction or make a decision about the allegations (Borgdorff, 2008). The victim will feel heard and validated when her church puts forth energy and time to determine the truth about what happened and how to respond properly to it.

The council/elder board should assign an advocate for the victim (as well as for the accused) so that she does not feel alone in the situation. An advocate can be a voice and support for the victim in church meetings, letter writings, and at hearings. The advocate can also be the liaison between the victim and the council, fact-finding panel, and other contacts as the allegations are investigated. The council should also assign a pastoral care person to the victim and her family (and to the accused and his family). Because the grievousness of the sin of betrayal by a church leader, the person appointed to serve in the pastoral care capacity should be competent, experienced, and skilled in pastoral care and not be member of the involved church. The church remains responsible for the spiritual welfare of the victim and her family. Involving a pastoral care person helps to address this responsibility.

Good communication can help the victim begin the forgiveness process. Church systems are notorious for poorly communicating with those who have been harmed by a church leader. One way to ensure that communication is present is to invite the victim to come to special meetings with the council so that the victim can share how she is doing and to see if there are additional concerns she would like to express. The victim can take her advocate and pastoral care person with her and she can share a letter of her concerns or communicate her concerns orally to the council. This provides time for the council to express their ongoing concern for her and to share a prayer time with her. This expression of love and compassion by the elders is a way to help the victim realize that the council cares deeply for her and can be encouraging to her through this difficult time. When the council validates her feelings, she begins to release her anger and the forgiveness process can begin.

And what if the church doesn't?

Victims, you already know that councils and elder boards don't want to deal with your allegations of abuse. Church leaders often don't understand abuse, and they don't like conflict. They typically respond by avoiding, dodging, ignoring, and denying that anything happened. Fearing their own ignorance about what to do and fearing their own reputations within the church community, they will do nearly anything to avoid you, and they pray that you will just go away.

Benyei et al. (2006) share their perspective on how church leaders should respond to accusations of abuse:

> How would people respond if a deranged bomber were to succeed in blowing up a building filled with innocent adults and children? And, after a long period of confusion and dithering by officials, who knew the bomber well, a single ambulance appeared to whisk away only the bomber? And, meanwhile, all direct victims, the family members of victims, and those in the wider community who were thoroughly traumatized by the event were left to fend for themselves?

> To summarize the old way of handling these cases, the offender was sent to treatment, given financial assistance, and often given a "geographical cure." The victim/survivor received at most a small financial settlement, often in return for silence. Because nothing

was revealed about the abuse, all those secondarily affected were ignored. Even if a case became public, no thought was given to the needs of the congregation.

In a more effective practice of triage, the old order is reversed, so that the needs of victims/survivors and all secondary victims take precedence over the needs of the offender. This new practice represents a radical change and can be expected to meet a lot of resistance. Of course, the offender does need assistance from the faith community, yet the others need more – much more. A just response for everyone must prevail if any religious tradition is to survive, even thrive, in good health (p. 3).

When the church refuses to address allegations of abuse by a church leader, the process of beginning forgiveness becomes complicated. Victims are being re-abused by the leaders' negligence. Church leaders who ignore your allegations of abuse are shaming you and hurting you; they represent an institution of harm rather than healing.

So how does one forgive the church when the church refuses to start the process? That is a difficult question with an unclear answer. Here are a few ideas:

1. Take the legal route if you can.
    In recent years, the public and the judicial system have become more concerned about abuse by church leaders. This concern has caused more states to allow victims to file civil suits against their offenders. In most instances, especially if the case involves sexual abuse or there is proof of damages because of the abuse, victims are winning cases. Usually attorneys will charge contingency fees, basing their fees on the amount of the settlement.
    Taking the legal route provides adequate protection

for the victim. The attorney who takes the case will shield the victim from the heat and anger of the opposing side and will advise and protect the victim. Churches don't like to be involved in litigation. Typically if a victim threatens to hire an attorney, the church will start to work with the victim to come to a solution that does not involve legal action.

However, keep in mind that the incident becomes a matter of public record once the law is involved. The media can access your public records and can print stories about your case. This loss of privacy can be painful.

Going the legal route provides justice. Just as when a church follows an investigative process, a victim's involving the law gets at truth, confronts the wrongdoer, and provides restitution for damages. The legal route can help the victim to begin the process of forgiving the church.

2. File a complaint with the abuser's licensing board or ministry board.

   If the church leader who abuses you is licensed in any way, contact and file a complaint against him with the organization who licensed him. Some church leaders have preaching licenses, others have counseling licenses, and some are affiliated with professional associations. Check the church leader's credentials, contact the organizations he is affiliated with, and request a form to file a grievance against one of their members.

3. Contact the liability insurance company for the pastor/church leader.

   Pastors and church leaders typically carry liability insurance. Find out who insures the offender and send a letter to the insurance company, explaining what the church leader did to you. Typically insurance companies become very concerned about possible allegations against one of the people they insure and will address the concerns with the church where it happened.

4. Address your complaint to a broader board that governs your church.

   If your direct elder board or council refuses to address your allegations of abuse, in some church structures, the allegations can go to a higher level of authority. In some denominations, this can be a regional church governing body or a supervisory denominational board. In your complaint, tell not only about the abuse experience you had, but also about the negligence of the direct governing board in addressing your allegations.

5. Seek out professional help.

   It's possible that none of the steps listed here will be an option for you. In some cases, the perpetrator has passed away, the church is no longer in existence, or those responsible refuse to allow you to proceed with allegations. If this happens, forgiveness is still possible, but you will have to seek out professional help.

   First, find a therapist who understands how to help victims of abuse work through the forgiveness process. Usually, therapists specialize in certain mental health issues. When you call a counseling agency, ask for a therapist who specializes in abuse and forgiving.

   Second, if you can, find a pastor who can provide spiritual counsel and direction in your journey to forgive. There are pastors, again, who are especially good at bringing healing to your soul and can find ways to connect you back to church if you wish. Be careful that this person does not pressure you to forgive quickly and also is gifted with being a good listener. He or she should have a caring heart about those who have been harmed by the church.

Third, there are many support groups online that can help you work through the hurt and anger about your abuse experience. Search out a group that may be a fit for you and give it a try. Your therapist or pastoral care person can also help you find an online support group or a local group if you are unsure where to go. Connecting with people who have had similar experiences can help greatly in the healing process.

With the exception of the last concern, these suggestions can lead to some sort of justice for you, the victim, and can be vital in helping the process of forgiving to begin.

Conclusion

When a church leader abuses, the governing authorities should do their part to make forgiveness for the victim possible. Accountability, thorough investigations, truth-seeking, and action are necessary for the victim to know and feel that the church cares about what happened to her. Should the church leaders be negligent and sloppy in their response to abuse allegations by a church leader, it becomes nearly impossible for the victim to forgive the church and the abuser. That negligence by the church becomes a serious offense against the victim.

Chapter 8
Forgiving: What the Victim Should Do

While they were stoning him, Stephen prayed, "Lord Jesus, receive my spirit." Then he fell on his knees and cried out, "Lord, do not hold this sin against them." When he had said this, he fell asleep.

—Acts 7:59–60

Trust is betrayed by the pastor. A person we thought would do what was best for everyone chose instead does wrong and harms those entrusted to him. Abuse by a pastor, no matter what kind of abuse it was—sexual assault, emotional/verbal abuse, physical abuse, or one of the lesser abuses—does harm. When abused by a church leader, the victim needs to address two layers of harm. One layer is the harm done by the actual wrongful behavior and the other layer is the fact that the abuse was done by a church leader.

The victim must think

As her shame surfaces, so do the "what ifs" as she decides what to do. What if what happened gets out? What will people think? What will it do to my name and reputation? What if

I'm not believed and I'm ostracized by my faith community? Can I still go to church? Will people talk to me? What if the council doesn't do anything about it? What if they laugh or tell me that I'm lying, then what? Is there some kind of process used when this kind of thing happens in our church? Where do I turn for help?

Smedes (1996) provides some thoughts about what forgiveness is *not*:

Forgiving someone who did us wrong does not mean that we tolerate the wrong he did.

Forgiving does not mean that we want to forget what happened.

Forgiving does not mean that we excuse the person who did it.

Forgiving does not mean that we take the edge off the evil that was done to us.

Forgiving does not mean that we surrender our right to justice.

Forgiving does not mean that we invite someone who hurt us once to hurt us again (p. 55–56).

Let's look at what Smedes (1996) says here and place it as best we can in the context of abuse by a church leader.

Never tolerate a pastor's abusive behavior

Nowhere in Scripture does it tell us to tolerate—to put up with—sin, especially a sin committed by a leader. Jesus confronted the self-righteous Pharisees and called them a brood of vipers, blind guides, and hypocrites (Matt. 23 NIV study Bible). Pastors who abuse are not fulfilling the mandate to serve their church and community. Putting up with their abusive behaviors is enabling sin to continue. Christians are to take a strong stand against such things.

Never forget a pastor's abuse

We can never forget the big things that happen to us. With time it is possible that the intensity of the memories will decrease and the emotional pain will diminish. But we do not forget. Smedes (1996) writes, "Forgiving does not edit bad things out of our memories anymore than it makes the bad things good. Forgiving only helps us remember the positive things that follow it." By remembering the bad that was done to you, you own who you are and where you come from. Your memory of the abuse will empower you to make sure it will never happen to you again.

Never "blow off" the abuse

We grow up with the belief that when bad things happen to us, we should "blow it off and tell ourselves we're okay." That approach is called "lying to yourself." When you have been abused by a church leader, you're not okay. You have been deeply wounded by someone who was trusted and thought to be a safe person. By blowing it off, you are in denial about what really happened to you and it is only a matter of time before you will have to face it. People who blow off the serious things in life become people who experience depression and anxiety and have hearts full of bitterness.

Never minimize the evil that was done to you

When abuse has happened, it's called abuse. As stated earlier, there are many kinds of abuse church leaders can commit. When abuse has happened to you, name it. Was it sexual abuse? Physical abuse? Breach of confidentiality? Undue influence? Whatever it is, name that abuse.

Justice must prevail

There's a reason we have a legal system. If you study our legal system, you will learn that much of it is based on the principles of the Bible. Justice is one of those principles. When a person robs a bank, he goes to jail. When someone drives drunk and kills someone, he goes to jail.

So it is with abusive pastors. When they abuse, justice—an attempt to make things as right as possible because of the harm done—is necessary. Without justice, our society would not survive. If there was no accountability for speeders or for those who assault, people could do anything to each other, with no fear of being punished. Our streets would be unsafe and protection from harm would be non-existent. Justice must win every time wrong is done. In the case of abusive pastors, justice must prevail.

Use your anger to prevent it from happening again

Anger is okay. How you express your anger can be an issue. In your anger, you are not to hurt yourself, others, or property. Anger, when controlled, can be a good thing. Anger says that a wrong was done and it was unfair. Anger gives us energy to take care of things, especially things that directly affect us. Anger prevents apathy and laziness and can motivate us to do things we wouldn't otherwise do. Anger protects us from being wronged again.

The victim must feel

Victim, are you willing to suffer? This is a very important question. In our society, we don't want to suffer. We want things to be good and we want to pretend everything is okay. We believe that we can handle anything that comes our way. We think we can forgive in a day. We think that being a Christian means that whatever happens to us, we forgive quickly and easily.

Many years ago, a nine-year-old girl was kidnapped, raped, and murdered. A few days later her family reported to the public that they forgave the killer. Really? I don't believe it. This is not forgiveness. This is about a family who doesn't want to own their pain and anger about what happened. This is a family who doesn't want to feel their feelings and face their suffering. This is a family who has never had to come face to face with a serious case of needing to forgive someone before. Forgiveness for something like this never comes in three days. It can take years.

Victim, are you willing to suffer? Are you willing to feel all of your feelings about the abuse that happened to you? Are you willing to be angry about what the pastor did to you? Can you identify your feelings of betrayal, mistrust, and confusion? Can you acknowledge that this really happened to you and you are greatly pained by it? Can you agonize over your abuse, express it to those who need to know, and admit how much it hurt you?

Forgiving can only be done by the victim. She was the one who was wronged. She is the one who has to forgive. Living through sleepless nights and anxious days, experiencing intense times of anxiety and panic, and bearing the pain by not being able to stop the crying, she is doing the hard work of suffering. She is remembering her losses. She thinks about a time when life use to be simple, when marriage and family life were a joy, and when the stressors of life were over little things. In her suffering, she wishes everything could be erased. She wishes that the abuse never happened or that it happened to someone else.

Processing all of your feelings and anger, talking out how much this has hurt you and your family, and crying every bit of sadness out will take a long time. I tell my clients and those abused by the church that it will take a generation to pass before forgiveness can happen. That is usually about twenty-five years.

Our cognitive self doesn't want to believe it will take that long. We think that we are good at forgiving and we can do it fast and easily. Although we may think this is true, our emotional side will tell it differently. Know that your cognitive and emotional sides run at different speeds. Our cognitive side can say what happened makes sense. I can cognitively forgive. But it won't feel like it.

The problem is that we cannot control our emotions. Emotions go at their own speed. That is why the family who said they could forgive the killer of their daughter three days after her death could cognitively do it, but emotionally they hadn't even begun the process. Allow time for your emotions to process your pain.

During this time, the victim may realize that she never really paid attention to what abuse was or what the dark side of leadership looked like. Now it seems that in nearly every newscast she hears or newspaper story she reads, there are stories about abuse or rape or assaults or church leaders having moral failure. She wonders why she never noticed this before. She questions whether she has been attentive enough to this important issue of our society and community.

Victim, you are to go there. You must go where you pain is greatest and process your feelings about the abuse. You are to stop the denial, ignoring, avoiding, and pretending about what happened to you. Admit to yourself you need help. Get into counseling. Talk to professionals. Find a support group. And talk and talk and talk about how much you hurt. Suffering and feeling are a part of the forgiving process.

The victim must do

When a church leader abuses someone, the victim must do things to address it. There are several ways victims can address the abuse, including taking the ecclesiastical route, taking the legal route, going through an investigative process, or in some cases, reporting the abuser to his licensing board or professional association.

When a victim does nothing in response to her abuse, she is taking the "helpless, poor me" approach. This approach will cause her to wallow in her grief, and her shame and feelings of helplessness will dominate her life. She will feel that the world controls her and that she has no control over her world. Without addressing the abuse, the pastor will continue on in his work—acting as if nothing has happened—which will increase her burden and cause her to be more despondent and angry. Doing nothing will hamper her ability to forgive the pastor.

In the forgiveness process, she will have to challenge herself and her church. When her church leaders give simplistic answers, she must challenge it and them to search more deeply for the difficult answers about what happened. She may hear things like "He's a family man, he'd never do that." "That happened several years ago. You wouldn't want to bring this all up now, would you?" "You are making a big deal out of this. You need to move on." The victim will need to challenge herself and church leaders.

Confronting the church when its leader abuses is intimidating work. And if they are blowing you off or ignoring you, be persistent. Stay with it. Keep knocking on their door and keep sending them your letters of concern, until you have their full attention. Forgiving is about getting at the full truth of what happened. Many leaders will feel inadequate and ill-equipped about what to do. Don't let that slow you down in confronting them. Don't excuse their excuses about not knowing what to do. In your approach, teach them about how painful your abuse has been. Teach them about what the effects of abuse have been for you and how your life is never going to be the same because of it.

When you challenge the church, you are showing that you will not tolerate wrongful behavior again. You are showing that you are never going to let your guard down again. You are going to ensure that others will never be hurt as you were. Doing is a part of the forgiveness process.

Helping yourself walk through the forgiveness process

To help in the forgiveness process, first buy books on forgiveness. If you're not sure what to read, ask your pastor or church leader for names of books. Next, three times a week, go to your church for prayer time and solitude. Pick a time when there are few people in the building so that you have privacy and your time at church will be uninterrupted. It may help to inform the church office what you are doing so your time alone is respected. Take your Bible and a book about forgiveness with you and sit in a pew in the sanctuary.

Remember that the first time you do this, it may be difficult. Your emotions and fears may overwhelm you. Old memories will resurface, anger will be stirred, and you will want to leave. Know that it's okay if this happens. This is some of the trauma that is resurfacing for you. If this feels too overwhelming for you, try it in smaller steps. You could meet in a classroom first or maybe just drive around the church building. You can do your prayer time in the car or in the classroom. Take it one small step at a time. Be patient with yourself and over time your visits to church will become easier.

While you are seated in the pew, look around the sanctuary. Bring to mind the things that once were precious to you. Remember the baptism of your children? Remember the times you led worship? Remember the times you helped out with Vacation Bible School? Let yourself remember.

Look at the cross in the front of church. Think about what it stands for and all of the love Jesus has for you. Remember the time you professed your faith, and think back to the time you promised God that you would do whatever He had planned for your life.

Open your Bible and read some of your favorite psalms. Recall how the writers were often distressed about their lives and thought God had abandoned them. Let your tears fall as you recite verses that speak to you and paraphrase the verses so you speak directly to God about your pain. As time goes by, continue to find passages to read, from both the Bible and your books, and spend part of your time in prayer. In your prayers, you may include telling God about your emotions related to the abuse, what feelings you have toward Him, and how you want to forgive but can't, and ask Him to soften your heart so you can. Keep a journal of the insights and answers He gives you. This can be done for as long as it is helpful for you. I suggest you try it for several months.

Letting others help you walk through the forgiveness process

Professional help is needed when you have been abused by a church leader. Having someone to talk to about your deepest hurts and feelings of betrayal is key to recovery and forgiveness. A therapist can help you to process your feelings and emotions. A pastoral care person can help with your spiritual needs. There are specialized support group services and online networks that specifically address clergy abuse issues. I encourage you to attend seminars and workshops that address the topic of abuse in the church and how to forgive the church.

Conclusion

Forgiveness is difficult. The process of forgiveness is messy. One day you may feel that you have let go of all of your anger and hurt. And the next day it comes right back. To forgive you must check your thinking, process your feelings, and do what needs to be done to have justice.

Forgiving a church leader who abused is hard work. It takes a lot of time, prayer, and patience. With God's help, you can do it.

Chapter 9
Putting it All Together:
Forgiving the Church

Get rid of all bitterness, rage and anger, brawling and slander, along with every form of malice. Be kind and compassionate to one another, forgiving each other, just as in Christ God forgave you.

—Ephesians 4:31–32

Putting it all together

We remember the church of our childhood. We recall the beliefs we had about church. We read about what abuse is and how it affects its victims. We learn about the different ways the church can abuse. We've read the stories of abuse by the church and we grieve and are saddened about how victims have suffered at the hands of the leadership. We see the importance of the church doing its part so that the process of forgiveness can begin for the victim. We know it's the victim who has been wronged, and it's the victim who must choose to forgive.

The victim stands at a fork in the road. Why should she go through the process of forgiveness? Why should she go through all of this work when she already has so much on her heart and mind? It's not fair that she has to do the work of forgiveness when she never asked for this to come into her life. Shouldn't the abuser be the one doing the work? Does she really have to forgive the church? Does she really have to forgive church leaders, when they're the ones who are supposed to know what they are doing, and they are the ones who are supposed to be safe? Why does she have to carry this burden? Why does the pastor get off so easily? She didn't ask for all of these problems. She wasn't the one who seduced the pastor. He's the one who did it to her.

So, why must the victim forgive a church leader who has abused? Here are some thoughts to help answer these difficult questions:

1. **Because God says so**
   "Forgive each other, just as in Christ God forgave you" (Eph. 4:32).

   "Forgive whatever grievances you may have against one another. Forgive as the Lord forgave you" (Col. 3:13).

   "Forgive and you will be forgiven" (Luke 6:37).

We need to wrestle with God about this. Forgiving a pastor or a church leader and forgiving the church is not easy. Forgiving the church is not simple. Forgiving the church is about letting yourself agonize over the pain and hurt that you have experienced and bit by bit giving all of it back to God. God wants us to forgive. He promises to help us forgive others, including the church leaders who have abused us. Entering a time of forgiveness is about committing and submitting to God, Scripture, time, and prayer. One day you will feel that you have forgiven, but the next day all of the anger and rage at what he did comes back. In this process, turn it over to God. Ask him to take your rage away and to give you back a heart that can forgive. Fall on your knees, cling to His promises, and plead for His strength to help you forgive.

2. So the abuse stops abusing

Forgiving helps stop the abuse from abusing. It's bad enough it happened once. Why would you cling to the memories of this evil and let it control your life? When you don't forgive, abuse controls you. You are not controlling it. Your rage, anger, sarcasm, and cynicism will destroy friendships and family relationships.

Smedes, in his book *Forgive and Forget*, says:

> The only way to heal the pain that will not heal itself is to forgive the person who hurt you. Forgiving stops the reruns of pain. Forgiving heals your memory as you change your memory's vision. When you release the wrongdoer from the wrong, you cut a malignant tumor out of your inner life. You set a prisoner free, but you discover that the real prisoner was yourself (p. 133).

3. Acceptance of reality heals

The truth is that your belief as a child that church leaders always knew what to do isn't true. Those church leaders who wore black suits and white shirts, and who came out of the consistory door, aren't much different from you and me. Today's church leaders mostly know how to be accountants, bankers, teachers, or plumbers. Their backgrounds and training do not help them to understand abuse and the effects of abuse by a church leader.

Most church leaders don't know what to do when their pastor abuses. Most church leaders fear taking a stand for the victim and confronting the abuser. They worry about hurting the pastor, or fear that they won't be liked by the pastor, or worry that addressing the abuse issues may divide the church. Most lack the training and education to respond to an abusive church leader, causing their response to be sloppy and careless. Members of church councils fear that their own names and reputations will be sullied, and they don't want that to happen. So, instead, they choose to minimize, deny, or ignore what victims are telling them. Sadly, I have seen this many times.

Accepting the reality that many times council members don't know how to respond to abuse helps you to reduce your expectations of how they will respond. This is not to excuse council members from knowing. But it helps to see them as church leaders with limited understanding and knowledge about what to do when a representative of the church abuses.

4. So bitterness is prevented

Bitterness is an ugly thing. Bitterness is an ungodly thing. When you don't forgive, your anger turns into bitterness. Bitterness is when it's no longer anger or rage. It's more like hate. Bitterness does not enhance relationships but ends them. It's difficult to have fellowship with a bitter person. If you don't forgive, one of the things you lose is being in healthy relationships with others. Bitterness always wins; this makes you, the victim, the loser.

5. Because it's what's best for us.

When a church leader abuses, our lives come crashing down and we don't know where to go or what to do. When all of the investigations are complete and when nothing else can be done to bring about justice, we need to look at all that has happened and realize that the last thing to do is to forgive. When we choose to forgive, we do it for ourselves (Smedes, 1996, p. 71). We are like a bird who lived in a cage with clipped wings, and forgiveness opens the cage door, forgiveness gives us new wings, and forgiveness gives us new hope and new life for the days ahead. When we forgive, we leave the cage of oppression, hurt, and evil. Our flight is about leaving the hurt behind and flying toward better days and brighter tomorrows. With God leading us, we experience relief, comfort, and guidance, for we know that He can and will heal; He says, "The sun of righteousness will rise with healing in its wings. And you will go out and leap" (Malachi 4:2), and, "I carried you on eagles' wings and brought you to myself" (Exodus 19:4).

And Isaiah tells us, "But those who hope in the Lord will renew their strength. They will soar on wings like eagles; they will run and not grow weary, they will walk and not be faint" (40:31).

Smedes (1996) asserts, "It must be healed before we can do anyone else any good at all. It is as simple as that: Forgiving has to heal our pain before it can heal anybody else's pain" (p. 73).

In other words, abuse must be healed before we can do anyone else any good at all. It is as simple as that: Forgiving has to heal our abuse before we can help heal anybody else's abuse.

Conclusion

What suffering there is when someone has been abused by the church. What a hard thing it is to forgive the church. For some, the childhood beliefs about church are destroyed when they are abused as adults. For others, their understanding of church was distorted and confused when they were children because of the bad things done to them.

I grieve with you. I am angered at what happened to you. I never excuse abusive pastors and church leaders who abuse. I believe in holding them fully accountable, whether that means calling in legal authorities, reporting the abuse to the ecclesiastical authorities, filing complaints and allegations to professional associations to which they may be members, and/ or bringing the charges through the entire hierarchy of church government to ensure enough has been done.

As a Christian, I believe the church and all believers have

a responsibility to God to do all that we can to bring our fallen brother to accountability, discipline, and even punishment. This is done with the hope and prayer that the abuser will have remorse and sorrow for what he did and that he will turn away from his sin.

If we are really his brothers and sisters in Christ, if we really take our membership seriously, if we believe that we should confront and love our brother, if we are invested in doing all that is good for our leadership when it does wrong, then we are accountable to God to ensure that all is done to address our brother and the abuse he has committed.

And if we want our sister to know our support and love for her, if we want our sister to have the proper understanding of how the church brings healing and not harm to its members, and if we believe that we are responsible for making it possible for the victim to begin the process of forgiving the church, then we are accountable to God to ensure that all is done to address the allegations of abuse so she can begin the forgiveness process.

And with God's help, the proper church response to abuse will do more than just begin the forgiveness process for the victim. It will become the foundation that helps the victim continue on in the forgiveness process until total and complete forgiveness can occur.

Things are not well with his soul when the pastor abuses. Go after it, church members and leaders, for that is what God calls us to do.

Bibliography

Ainscough, C., & Toon, K. (2000). *Surviving Childhood Sexual Abuse*. Cambridge, MA: Da Capo Press.

Allender, D. B. (1990). *The Wounded Heart*. Colorado Springs, CO: Navpress.

Benyei, C. R., Frampton, E.L., Hopkins, N.M., Liberty, P.L., and Pope-Lance, D. (2006). *When a Congregation is Betrayed: Responding to Clergy Misconduct*. Herndon, VA: The Alban Institute.

Borgdorff, P. (2008). *Manual of Christian Reformed Church Government*. (Rev. ed.). Grand Rapids, MI: Faith Alive Christian Resources.

Department of Commerce Office of Crime Victims Advocacy (n.d.). *Sexual Assault*. Retrieved from: http://www.commerce.wa.gov/site/261/default.aspx.

Fortune, M.M., and Poling, J.N. (1996). *Sexual Abuse by Clergy: A Crisis for the Church*, Decatur, IL: Journal of Pastoral Care Publications, Inc.

GRACE Amended Final Report for the Investigatory Review of

Child Abuse at New Tribes Fanda Missionary. (2010, August 28). Retrieved from www.fandaeagles.com.

Johnson, D. and Van Vonderen, J. (1991). *The Subtle Power of Spiritual Abuse.* Minneapolis, MN: Bethany House Publishers.

Mersch, J. (n.d.) *Child Abuse.* Retrieved from http://www. medicinenet.com/child_abuse/page5.htm

National Center for Victims of Crime (2011). *Sexual Assault.* Retrieved from http://www/ncvc.org/ncvc/main.aspx?dbNam e=DocumentViewer&DocumentID=32369#1.

Newton, C.J. (2001, April). *Child Abuse: An Overview.* Retrieved from http://www.findcounseling.com/journal/ child-abuse/physical-abuse.html.

Smedes, L.B. (1984). *Forgive and Forget.* New York, NY: HarperSanFrancisco.

Smedes, L.B. (1996). *The Art of Forgiving.* Nashville, TN: Moorings.

Taylor, T.F. (1996). *Seven Deadly Lawsuits: How Ministers Can Avoid Litigation and Regulations.* Nashville, TN: Abingdon Press.

Winters, D. (2011, March 25). *PASTOR CHARGED: Former Pella church leader accused of sexually abusing four women.* Retrieved from http://www.whotv.com/who-story-pella-pastor-arrested-sexual-abuse-032511,0,7356330.story